S0-BYK-033

The World of
Europe

Consulting Editors
Revised Edition:

Karl A. Roider, Jr.
Frederic A. Youngs, Jr.

The World of

Europe

since 1815

David H. Pinkney
Amos E. Simpson
Vaughan B. Baker

Revised Edition

FORUM PRESS

Library of Congress Catalog Card Number: 78-67276

ISBN: 0-88273-332-X

First Printing January 1979

Cover Design by Jerry Moore and Janet Moody

Contents

Preface

The teaching of Western Civilization is enjoying a new lease on life in many colleges and universities today. The abandonment of its study that became so fashionable in the late 1960s and early 1970s has itself been abandoned. There were many cries for radical reform in those turbulent decades, but it became apparent that young people who did not realize how and why the institutions of society arose were ill-prepared to suggest meaningful reforms. The present, after all, is an extension of the past, and without an awareness of the experiences of earlier centuries, today's world is incomprehensible and tomorrow's doomed to repeating earlier mistakes.

The revised edition of *The World of Europe* is designed as a brief textbook with a balanced introduction to the main developments of Western society. The text has sufficient detail to reflect the complexity of the European experience, yet is concise enough to give the instructor great flexibility in combining the text with the other resources used in the course. There is first of all a narrative of important events from the earliest near-eastern civilizations to the end of 1978. Interwoven into this political schema are analyses of the full range of human achievements: governments fashioned to meet political needs, religions to serve spiritual ends, and economies and societies to form the arena in which European men and women lived, worked, and aspired. Furthermore there is consideration of the variety of cultural achievements — literary, intellectual, and artistic — which crowned European life. Because the text is relatively brief, it can serve not only for a study of the Western experience but also as an integral part of a wider study of world civilizations.

To the advantages of the original edition, the revised *World of Europe* adds a number of improvements. Over one-third of the original text has been completely rewritten, including two entirely new sections. DeLamar Jensen, Professor of History at Brigham Young University and author of the chapters on the sixteenth century, has contributed the new section on the Renaissance, and David Pinkney, Professor of History at the University of Washington, has written the chapters on the nineteenth century. The other authors have revised their sections to reflect recent interpretations and debates concerning the crucial events of Western history. New and pertinent illustrations have been added, without inflating the cost of the volumes.

While the changes in the revised edition have been designed to make the text even more useful, the flexibility of the original remains. The book is bound in one volume for one-semester or full-year courses, in two volumes for two-semester courses, and in three volumes for institutions on the quarter system. In addition to the two-volume set, which is divided into periods before and after 1715, there is a special volume for the years since 1500. The revised edition also features the popular 64-page minibooks, each a complete study of a major period in the Western experience. The minibooks can be used as core books in either Western or World Civilization courses or as supplementary reading for individual periods.

A number of scholars have made useful suggestions which contributed greatly to this revised edition: Professors Wayne C. Bartee of Southwest Missouri State University, James Brink of Texas Tech University, John B. Cameron, Jr., of the University of Southwestern Louisiana, James Chastain of Ohio University, John B. Henneman of the University of Iowa, Peter J. Klassen of California State University-Fresno, Reynold S. Koppel of Millersville State College, and members of the faculty at Brigham Young University, including Douglas F. Tobler, George M. Addy, Peter M. Ascoli, Paul B. Pixton, K. Michael Seibt, and Malcolm Thorp. The authors also wish to express their appreciation to the staff of Forum Press for their assistance in the publication of this book, particularly to Erby M. Young, Managing Director of Forum Press, who developed both the original and revised editions, including the mini-book concept, and supported the authors throughout all stages.

Frederic A. Youngs, Jr.
Karl A. Roider, Jr.
General Editors

THE NINETEENTH CENTURY
1815-1914

16

The Aftermath of Upheaval

THE CENTURY THAT BEGAN IN 1815 and ended in 1914 has been called "The Great Century." In no preceding century had there been such growing mastery over nature, such a lavish outpouring of material goods, such an increase in liberty, such rising participation in political power, such spreading of education, and such confident hope of the approaching end of ignorance, poverty, and oppression. It was a century of rapid and unprecedented change and Europeans, especially urban western Europeans, in the closing decades of the century, lived in a world different from that of their great-grandparents only eighty or a hundred years earlier.

But historians, though at first attracted by change, also find important elements of continuity in the century. Even in the west in 1914, not everyone was integrated into the urban, industrial economy, and tens of thousands did not share much of its rich productivity. In central, southern, and eastern Europe, large areas were still agrarian, culturally isolated, and little touched by the new technology. The church, despite spreading secularism and scepticism nurtured by a spectacular growth of science and an intensifying nationalism, was still a potent force, holding the loyalties of masses of men and women. The landed aristocracy was by no means ousted from places of power and influence. History, however, is above all concerned with change and so we will examine, without neglecting continuities, the great changes that came to the European world between 1815 and 1914.

● Social and Economic Conditions

The growth of population in the nineteenth century was almost explosive compared with growth in earlier centuries. Owing to an expanding food supply, improved sanitation, and better medical care, Europe's inhabitants doubled from 188 million to more than 400 million, and also furnished 18 million emigrants to other continents. The population boom came first to western Europe, then spread eastward, and everywhere in the course of the century, population began to shift out of rural areas and into towns and cities.

The growth and steady urbanization of Europe's population had its origins in the industrial revolution, which began in England. English manufacturing, already well into the industrial revolution by the end of the eighteenth century, and English commerce were also stimulated by the Napoleonic Wars. After 1815 industrialization came to central and eastern Europe. By the 1880s most major governments were faced with such consequences of industrialization as overcrowded and polluted cities, urban crime, and the threat of social revolution.

The industrialization of Europe affected many established patterns of trade. Britain shipped her low-cost cotton goods and advanced machinery into ever larger markets around the world. Russia became an important exporter of wheat to western European urban markets. In the 1840s Prussia completed the organization of most of Germany excluding Austria into a customs union that brought the benefits of a large free trade area to German manufacturers and traders a quarter of a century before the formation of the German Empire. The introduction of new technology – steam-driven iron and then steel ships on the high seas, and railroads penetrating into the frontier areas of the world in the latter half of the century – opened the Great Plains of North America, the pampas of South America, and the back country of Australia to European goods.

● Liberalism and Socialism

The Industrial Revolution spawned two influential schools of thought on the organization of the economy, society, and government –

liberalism and socialism.

"Liberal" and "liberalism" are so corrupted by use and misuse that today they no longer have precise meaning, but during much of the nineteenth century their meanings were clear to contemporaries. As the name suggests, "liberals" were men who believed in liberty. The political liberties that they advocated included the basic personal civil liberties – freedom of speech, freedom of the press, and freedom of assembly – and self-government through representative parliaments but with the government's powers clearly defined and limited by a constitution. They were not democrats; they believed in government by the competent, and for them competence was established by the ownership of property. Liberal economic thought held that individual freedom unrestricted by government regulation would assure maximum productivity and best serve the common good. This concept of *laissez-faire* originally developed in reaction against the mercantilist regulations of the seventeenth and eighteenth centuries, but it was commonly used to justify, in the name of the common good, bans on the organization of labor and on strikes. The liberals believed that in society the educated middle class of business and the professions should occupy or at least share the highest ranks. And they were antirevolutionary. The French Revolution and Napoleon had provided the legal and institutional foundations for a liberal society and economy, and all necessary change could be achieved by peaceful, political means.

The socialists shared the liberals' enthusiasm for the productive potential of the new industrial economy, but they were less interested in liberty than in justice, especially the just and equitable distribution of the fruits of industry. Liberty, they held, bred not justice but exploitation, the enrichment of a few and the impoverishment of the many, and led to the concentration of economic power in the hands of a few magnates. It produced monetary crises and economic depressions, unemployment and insecurity. The prescriptions of the socialists varied from school to school and from individual to individual, but most agreed on the replacement of private ownership of the means of production – the land, mines, railroads, and factories – with social ownership, and the replacement of *laissez-faire* with planning and direction by society. One of the government's primary responsibilities, in the view of the socialists, was to assure equitable distribution of the economy's product. The early utopian socialists, confident in the goodness of man, believed that these ends would be achieved if man's natural inclination to cooperate were allowed expression, and they proposed to organize men into communities that would permit cooperation to prevail. On the other hand, Karl Marx and the scientific socialists in the second quarter of the century rationally analyzed the liberal capitalist economy, exposed its weaknesses, and worked out a formula by which it would be replaced, in a process they assumed was both revolutionary and inevitable, by a socialist economy and a classless society. In the latter half of the century it was Marxism that became the prevailing socialist doctrine.

• The Vienna Congress and Metternich's System

Although liberalism and socialism would animate many of the century's reforms, it was conservatism and fear of further revolution that dominated its first half. The final fall of Napoleon in 1815 ended a quarter century of almost continuous war and of intermittent revolution. War and revolution had produced such an upheaval of the old Europe that an international congress seemed essential to give the continent a new, stable organization. Representatives of the great powers and petitioners for the small met in Vienna in September 1814. The Vienna settlement, concluded the next year, defined power relationships sufficiently well to give Europe an entire century free of general European war. For the next hundred years European diplomacy revolved around decisions made or evaded at Vienna.

The delegates to the full congress were lavishly entertained by the imperial court and by the Austrian aristocracy, and the congress met only once – to ratify the final treaty. Most of the work was done by representatives of the four victorious powers. The leading figure was the Austrian foreign minister, Prince Clemens von Metternich. He together with Tsar Alexander I of Russia, King Frederick William III of Prussia, and the Duke of Wellington and Viscount Castlereagh, England's foreign secretary, together with the statesmen's assistants aided by some consultation with spokesmen of secondary states, made the basic decisions. The irrepressible Prince Talleyrand, the head of the French delegation, contrived to exploit disagreements among the victors to win a place for France in the deliberations.

The peacemakers came to Vienna with a shared antipathy to Napoleon and to the commitments made in several agreements concluded during the war. Their first objective was to secure themselves and their neighbors against renewed French aggression. The principle of legitimacy was to govern the filling of vacant or contested thrones; legitimate (that is, pre-revolutionary) monarchs were to be restored whenever possible. Talleyrand had devised and advocated this principle to assure the restoration of the Bourbons in France. Some powers expected specific rewards for their contribution to the struggle against the French. Out of

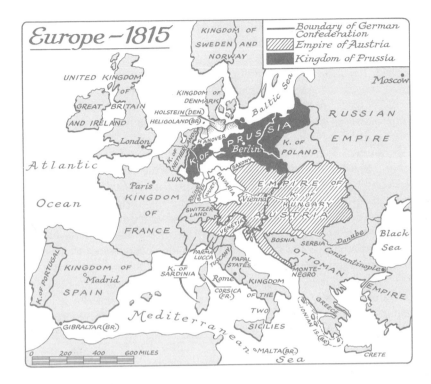

the conflicting demands the principals devised settlements embodied in the final act of the congress approved in June 1815.

• The Vienna Settlement

France emerged from her defeat with only light retribution. She was required to pay a modest indemnity and submit to a limited occupation until it was paid. Her boundaries were reestablished essentially as they were before the outbreak of the Revolutionary Wars. Fortunately for France, anti-French feeling concentrated largely on Napoleon; the Bonapartes were banned from all European thrones in the future. As barriers against French aggression the Kingdom of Sardinia was restored and enlarged by the addition of the Republic of Genoa, and the Kingdom of the Netherlands was strengthened by the annexation of the Belgian provinces, the prewar Austrian Netherlands. These two buffer states would slow or stop a French move toward the lower Rhine or into northern Italy. Prussia acquired the Rhine Province on the west bank of the Rhine and with it "the watch of the Rhine" against French aggression into middle Germany. Legitimate monarchs, Bourbons, were restored in France, in Spain, and in Naples, but the principle of legitimacy was not everywhere applied. Napoleon had merged hundreds of small German states into larger ones, and the congress accepted most of these changes. In Sweden the former French marshal, Jean Bernadotte, retained his succession to the throne. Sweden gave up Finland to Russia but acquired Norway. Austria lost the Belgian Netherlands but recovered her former Italian lands and also acquired Lombardy and Venetia in northern Italy and the former French Illyrian Province on the east shore of the Adriatic. The British recovered Hanover and picked up a few more colonies, including Malta and the Cape Colony. The Netherlands gained the Belgian provinces as compensation for the loss of the Cape Colony and Ceylon. In place of the Holy Roman Empire, a victim of the French Revolution and Napoleon, the congress created the Germanic Confederation composed of thirty-nine sovereign states under the presidency of Austria.

The most serious disagreement arose over Tsar Alexander's proposal to restore the Kingdom of Poland under Russian control. Prussia had acquired large areas of Poland in the partitions of the eighteenth century and had lost them after her defeat by Napoleon. Under the principle of legitimacy these lands should have been returned to Prussia; failing this, she should have been given compensatory territories elsewhere. Austria and Britain were concerned to prevent Russia's further penetration into central Europe and preferred that Prussia recover her Polish lands, but Frederick William of Prussia and many Prussian nationalists wanted to add Saxony to the Hohenzollerns' holdings, for it would round out Prussian territory and go far toward giving Prussia the leading position in Germany. Metternich opposed the latter solution and won Britain and France to his side, and for a time the dispute threatened to disrupt the congress. In the end a compromise gave Russia most of Poland but left some Polish lands to Prussia and Austria. Prussia acquired the northern half of Saxony and, reluctantly, the Rhine Province on the west bank opposite France. By these territorial shuffles Prussia became more German, exchanging most of her Polish subjects for German subjects, and was obliged to assume the lead in the defense of Germany against renewed French aggression on the middle Rhine. Against her will she was being pushed into a position of German national leadership.

The settlement paid scant attention to the ominously emerging, French-inspired nationalism in much of Europe, especially in Italy, Germany, Spain, and the Balkans. The intention of the peacemakers in Vienna was to restore as much as possible the Europe of 1789.

• The Aftermath of the Congress

To assure enforcement of the settlement, the victorious powers, Russia, Austria, Prussia, and Britain, joined in the Quadruple Alliance and committed themselves to police the agreements for twenty years and to meet regularly in congresses to discuss common problems. Tsar Alexander, at the time very much committed to Christian pietism, persuaded all his brother monarchs except George III of England to join a Holy Alliance, and to promise to be guided by Christian principles in dealing with each other and with their subjects.

One immediate consequence of the settlement was that the reactionary political views of the Habsburgs and the Austrian bureacracy came to dominate much of Germany. Reforms instituted or inspired by the French were stopped or in some cases reversed. A system of political spies and thought-control was instituted to eradicate liberal ideas. The Carlsbad Decrees of 1819 required member states of the Germanic Confederation to take repressive measures against liberals and liberal doctrines, and at the Congress of Troppau (1819) the three conservative monarchies agreed to the principle of intervention in other states to forestall or to stop revolutions. Metternich had posed as the spokesman of the rights of small states when opposing Prussia's annexation of Saxony, but now he argued for and obtained authority to intervene in the affairs of these same small states.

At a meeting at Aix-la-Chapelle in 1818 France joined the other powers in what then became the Quintuple Alliance. A number of minor problems were settled at Aix, and the so-called Congress System seemed to be working well. Meetings at Troppau in 1820, Laibach in 1821, and Verona in 1822, however, brought on the gradual disenchantment of Britain and the end of her cooperation with the Alliance. This in turn encouraged Russia, Prussia, and Austria to draw closer together. On the other side Britain and on occasion Bourbon France withheld support of Metternich's reactionary policies, but Metternich was scarcely hindered by their disapproval. In 1822 he won the Tsar's agreement to unilateral Austrian intervention to suppress uprisings in Italy and at the same time convinced Alexander not to intervene militarily in the Danubian Provinces of the Ottoman Empire on Russia's southern flank. Against Metternich's effective conservative leadership, liberalism made little progress in the decade after 1815.

• Russia

After 1815 the governments of most European states pursued domestic policies compatible with the conservative ideas that Metternich promoted internationally. The Russia of Alexander I was a bastion of rigid, authoritarian rule. Alexander had begun his reign with considerable sympathy for liberal ideas, but he had grown conservative, and his principal counsellor, Count Alexei Arakcheev, a brutal reactionary, easily countered the tsar's infrequent lapses into liberalism. Earlier limited steps toward the reduction of serfdom (a law promulgated in 1803 led to the freeing of 37,000 serfs in twenty years) were not pursued. Society remained rigidly hierarchical. Alexander's early interest in constitutional reform and limiting autocracy was forgotten, and the tsar's power grew ever more arbitrary. The bureaucracy was corrupt and ineffectual against Russia's massive problems. After 1816 a handful of educated nobles, many of whom had had their eyes opened by army service in western Europe after 1812, formed secret organizations to prepare reforms, but they were not only few in number but were also divided among themselves between constitutional monarchists and republicans.

In three border areas Alexander's rule was more enlightened. The Poles were permitted their own Kingdom of Poland, joined to Russia only by a personal union, and were allowed considerable autonomy in the management of their own affairs. Finland, which Russia had acquired in 1809, was similarly allowed a substantial degree of self-government. In the Baltic Provinces, Estonia, Kurland, and Livonia, Alexander liberated the serfs, not so much out of liberal conviction, but to win the local peasants to Russia and away from their masters, who were Baltic Germans.

• Austria

In Austria after 1815, Francis I and the bureaucracy stood resolutely opposed to change. The development of any organized movement for reform was forestalled by censorship, the surveillance of police spies, and drastic punishments. Even so powerful a figure as Metternich had to limit his effective activities to foreign affairs; he and a few others saw the need for some reform, but they were unable to change the ultra-conservative views of the emperor. High tariffs hampered the growth of trade and industry, and this prevented the development of a large and influential middle class which would have demanded reform of the antiquated regime. The German nobility of Austria administered and controlled a polyglot empire whose integrity was beginning to be threatened by the growing nationalisms of its subject peoples. Poles, Czechs, Hungarians, Serbs, Croats, Slovenes, and Italians were affected by nationalistic ideas which resulted from the French Revolution, and they increasingly resented Viennese rule.

In other German states Austrian diplomacy and influence imposed on Germany Francis's outmoded social and political values. In Austrian Italy, the Papal States, and the Kingdom of Naples the same conservative ideas and policies were imposed or encouraged, indirectly and unintentionally instilling anti-Austrian feeling and encouraging Italian nationalist sentiment throughout the peninsula.

● Prussia

After Prussia's disastrous defeat at the hands of Napoleon in 1806, King Frederick William III had consented to a series of far-reaching liberal and military reforms, and after 1815 German liberals hoped that Prussia would continue on this course and offer a lead to all Germany. But Frederick William had never given up his conservative convictions, and when the immediate danger from the French had passed, he had little interest in further change. Prince Frederick von Hardenberg, one of the principal architects of the great reforms, remained as chancellor but was frustrated in his efforts to give Prussia a parliament with some control over taxation, and he even had to retreat on some of his earlier reforms. In 1819 he was forced from office, and in the succeeding years the landed aristocracy tightened their hold on the civil government while continuing to dominate the socially arrogant officer corps. Even before Hardenberg's fall, Frederick William had come to share Metternich's fear of liberal ideas in Germany, and in 1819 they cooperated to win the approval of the Germanic Confederation for the Carlsbad Decrees, which required the German states to establish strict controls over teaching in the universities, to ban student organizations, and to censor the press. The educated middle class continued to hold some liberal ideas, and many of them occupied high posts in the civil service, but they tended to believe more in enlightened administration than in a constitution or a parliament as the key to progress. The one great liberal accomplishment of the immediate post-1815 decades was not in politics or society but in the economy. In 1818 the government abolished all internal tariffs in Prussia and then went on to extend this customs union, the *Zollverein*, to include most of non-Austrian Germany.

● Spain

In Spain under the restored Bourbon, Ferdinand VII, the conservative repression was unmatched in its severity and obscurantism. During the French occupation the Cortes, the national parliament, had drafted and approved a liberal constitution that abolished the Inquisition and the remains of feudalism, proclaimed the Rights of Man, and established a limited monarchy with a representative parliament. When Ferdinand regained his throne in 1814, he suspended the constitution, disbanded the Cortes, and undertook with the support of the army and the church the elimination or repression of all moderate and liberal influences in Spain. His oppressive and incompetent rule and his loss of the American empire, however, turned army officers against him, and in 1820 a revolt led by army officers forced him to restore the constitution and the Cortes. He appealed to the great powers for help, and in 1822 the Congress of Verona approved French intervention in Spain. The French invasion was little more than a triumphal march through the country, the mass of whose people were loyal to church and throne and suspicious of liberals. Ferdinand recovered his former powers and began a savage repression. Torture, imprisonment, and exile were the fate of thousands of Spanish liberals.

• France

In France after Waterloo the restored Louis XVIII understood that there could be no turning back to the pre-revolutionary regime, and he kept the forces of reaction and revenge under reasonable but not complete control. He granted the Charter of 1814, the most advanced constitution in Europe at the time; it established a parliamentary monarchy and reaffirmed the essential reforms of the Revolution and the empire. His most difficult task was to restrain the ultra-royalist, returned émigrés, who had an influential leader in the king's brother, the Count of Artois. Immediately after Napoleon's defeat at Waterloo the ultra-royalists in the south started the vengeful White Terror against his supporters. Two or three hundred Bonapartists or suspected Bonapartists were killed, and hundreds of others assaulted or jailed. The occupying powers feared that an excessive reaction might provoke the French to renewed revolution, and they aided Louis in ending the ascendancy of the extremists. After 1816 France enjoyed four years of moderate government by the constitutionalists, but the ultra-royalists had not given up. In 1820 the assassination by a republican of the Duke of Berry, heir presumptive to the throne, and the election to the Chamber of Deputies of the Abbé Gregoire, who had voted for the execution of Louis XVI in 1793, won them more support from both voters and deputies. For the remainder of Louis' reign and throughout the reign of his successor, Charles X, the former Count of Artois, the government was reactionary and pro-clerical. It was this conservative France that, to the dismay of liberals, sent an army to restore absolute monarchy in Spain in 1823. Superficially France seemed to be in step with the reactionary monarchies of southern and eastern Europe, but unlike them France had a substantial and articulate middle class, and it, and many from the aristocracy as well, saw their interests inseparably bound up with the liberal application of the Charter of 1814. Charles' and his ministers' failure to appreciate the strength of this conviction led to revolution in 1830.

• Britain

In Britain after 1815 as on the Continent, the dominant political orientation was conservative. The conservative Tories enjoyed the prestige of having led the nation to victory in the long struggle with Napoleon, and they were not sympathetic to change. The Corn Law of 1815, while it protected the predominately conservative agricultural landlords from the competition of cheap foreign grain, kept bread prices high. Poor harvests drove prices higher and added to popular distress. When desperate subjects resorted to violence, the government responded with repressive legislation, limiting the freedom of assembly and providing increased and speedier punishments for sedition. At Manchester in 1819, a troop of soldiers brutally dispursed demonstrators. By 1822, however, the fear of sedition had subsided, and more liberal elements had come into the leadership of the Tory party. The government then effected a number of reforms, especially in the law. The number of crimes punishable by death was cut from about two hundred to one hundred, and the strict laws forbidding workers to organize were somewhat relaxed. In the economic sector, some tariffs were reduced.

• The Romantic Movement

As conservatism dominated politics in the first half of the century, so romanticism dominated literature and the fine arts, and influenced political thought as well. As a broad movement it may be viewed as a reaction against the eighteenth-century Enlightenment and against the rationalism and classicism associated with it. Romantic literature was already well-established in England and Germany by the turn of the century, but in the first two or three decades of the new century the romantic movement was given potent impetus by the revulsion against the French Revolution, which seemed to many contemporaries to have demonstrated that the end result of the Enlightenment and its rationalism was violence, oppression, and cruelty.

In literature and the fine arts romanticism was specifically a rebellion against formalism and rules of artistic expression, a rebellion against rational analysis. The romantics wanted to *believe* not to *analyze*. Truth, they thought, was to be discovered not by reason but by intuition. "Beauty is truth, truth beauty, that is all/ Ye know on earth, and all ye need to know," wrote John Keats in 1819. The romantics denied the existence of any permanent forms or standards of beauty, any symbols that were eternally meaningful in all ages. Consequently, they rejected the rules of drama that had been accepted in the preceding centuries; they turned away from order and precision in music and from careful craftsmanship and subdued color in painting. They believed in freedom of expression. Each individual writer and artist must look to his own emotions for inspiration and frankly express his own feelings.

The Enlightenment had celebrated man's growing mastery over nature. The romantics celebrated unspoiled and unmastered nature. Romantic poets wrote passionately beautiful verse on the beauties of nature, Percy Bysshe Shelley's "To a Skylark," and Josef von Eichendorf's "Mondnacht," for example. Some discovered in the contemplation of nature mystical insights that reason could never offer. Painters found subjects in landscapes and seascapes and tried to capture their majesty in exaggerated forms.

The romantic painters filled their canvases with bright colors and slashing action. Their paintings were full of emotion, and they stirred emotions in viewers. Eugéne Delacroix's vivid and moving "Liberty Leading the People" (1830) was thought to be so inflammatory that it was removed from the galleries of the Louvre in the latter 1830s. Romantic composers used larger orchestras and more sophisticated instruments (the valve trumpet was invented about 1815) to produce music which by its rich, complex, and often clashing sounds and by its emotional appeal contrasted with the ordered, rational, elegant compositions of the eighteenth century. One need only listen successively to an eighteenth-century symphony or concerto by Mozart or Hayden and then to a nineteenth-century symphony by Beethoven or Berlioz to appreciate that music had entered a new age. In the latter half of the century the musical dramas of Richard Wagner were the ultimate expression of romanticism in music.

The men of the Enlightenment, confident of the perfectibility of man and of the promise of progress, had looked ahead to the golden age.

The romantic writers by contrast looked back to a golden age in the Middle Ages, a period which the Enlightenment had scorned. Sir Walter Scott wrote immensely popular historical novels about medieval knights and ladies. Victor Hugo took medieval Paris as his subject in *Notre-Dame de Paris* (1831). Architecture, too, championed medieval expressions. The nineteenth-century romantics revived Gothic architecture with its soaring, mystical, otherworldly features, a marked departure from the earth-bound and easily comprehensible forms of classical and baroque architecture of the previous century. Classical architecture was never entirely displaced, but the Gothic revival left its monuments across Europe: the British Houses of Parliament, begun in 1840 and completed in 1868, St. Pancras Station in London (1865), the Church of Sainte-Clotilde in Paris (1856), the completed Cologne Cathedral, and a scattering of pseudo-medieval castles.

The romantics were distinguished, too, by their interest in people. A favorite subject in romantic literature was the noble savage, the natural man or woman, uncorrupted by civilization. American Indians were often cast in this role, as in François-René Chateaubriand's *Atala* (1801) and Henry Wadsworth Longfellow's *Hiawatha* (1855). The romantic hero was another creation of the movement. He was the great man unfettered by convention and possessed of the strength, the imagination, and the will to accomplish great deeds. Napoleon was the inspiration of much of this thinking. He was the hero personified, and he had a special appeal after 1815, when his tyrannies began to fade, for he contrasted so sharply with emerging bourgeois leaders immersed in counting and technology. A contrasting romantic hero was popularized by Lord Byron, the rebel against society's conventions who is so locked in melancholy that he can do nothing to alter a tragic fate. Alexander Pushkin's *Eugene Onegin* (1826) is an example in Russian romantic literature.

For some the hero was not an individual but an idealized version of a whole people. The German philosopher Johann von Herder had, toward the end of the eighteenth century, planted the seminal idea that true culture issues not from the educated elite but only from the *Volk*, the ordinary people, and he held that every *Volk* had something valuable to contribute to civilization. This idea emerged in Jules Michelet's *Histoire de France* (1833-67), in which he glorified the French people, not French kings or military commanders, as the hero of the nation's history. Similarly the Slavophils in Russia, those who emphasized the oriental, non-western values in Russian life, extolled the Russian peasant as the source of Russia's unique contribution to civilization.

About mid-century romanticism began to give way to realism as the dominating force in the arts. The emerging realist writers and artists took their subjects from everyday life, not from an idealized past; their characters and figures were neither classical types nor romantic heros, but ordinary people depicted as they actually appeared to the artists. Gustave Flaubert's *Madame Bovary* (1857), George Eliot's *Adam Bede* (1859) and Ivan Turgenev's *Fathers and Sons* (1860) reveal the changing taste and standards in fiction; Gustave Courbet's "The Burial at Ornans" (1850) and Honoré Daumier's "Third Class Railway Carriage" (1862), in painting.

Romanticism had no exclusive and enduring affiliation with any particular political party or tendency of its time. At the outset of the nineteenth century it was usually associated with conservatism, an association that reflected its origins in rebellion against the eighteenth century. Chateaubriand, for example, one of France's greatest romantic writers, was active in the politics of the Restoration as an ultra-royalist. In the latter 1820s, however, the romantic allegiance generally shifted to the left, to the liberalism associated in France with the Revolution of 1830. Delacroix celebrated that revolution in his "Liberty Leading the People," one of the greatest of romantic paintings. The early French socialists of the 1830s and 1840s stood in the romantic tradition by their faith in the goodness of natural man before he was corrupted by institutions. In Germany romanticism was linked with the liberal nationalist movement by its emphasis on traditional folk culture and its glorification of the German past. But the conservative strand in romanticism continued, too. It may be seen in the person of Frederick William IV of Prussia, whose political policies were clearly influenced by his romantic veneration of the Christian-German Middle Ages. The early Slavophils in Russia were conservative romantics in their praise of Russian folk culture and their rejection of the ideas and institutions of Western liberalism, which were dear to their rivals, the Westerners.

• Revolt in Spanish America and in Greece

The system of great power cooperation through periodic congresses to preserve the Vienna settlement of 1815 disintegrated under the impact of independence movements in South America and in Greece. After 1808 much of South and Central America revolted against Spanish rule, and Britain and the United States, both hoping to win Spanish markets in these areas, encouraged the rebels. Had the principles of the Quadruple Alliance been followed, the European powers would have helped Spain to recover her colonies, but Britain refused to support such a policy and appeared to be ready to oppose its application by force. In 1823 President Monroe of the United States warned that North and South America were no longer "subjects for future colonization by European powers," and Britain's sympathy with the Monroe Doctrine, when coupled with the power of the Royal Navy, put teeth in the young nation's bold warning to the Old World. By 1829 all of Spain's American possessions, except Cuba and Puerto Rico, were independent of the government in Madrid.

In 1821 a Greek secret revolutionary society that had enjoyed Russian support, Russia having long been interested in expanding into the Balkan peninsula, launched a revolt against Turkish rule and appealed to Russia for help. Tsar Alexander had been convinced by Metternich, however, of the perils of encouraging revolution, and he refused to provide assistance. The revolt spread, nonetheless, over the Morea and to the Aegean islands. The Turkish government reacted vigorously and sometimes savagely to suppress and destroy the rebels. The Greek cause aroused immense sympathy among western Europeans and Americans, who saw the rebelling Greeks as the descendants of the ancient Greeks to whom western civilization owed so much. They regarded the rebels as classical Greeks again fighting Asiatic barbarians. Moreover, they were Christians, and the Turks were heathens. The revolt presented the governments of the great powers with an embarrassing dilemma. The Sultan of Turkey was a legitimate ruler, and by the principle of legitimacy he should be aided in his efforts to hold his lands against revolutionary subjects. On the other hand, the Greek Christians surely should not be abandoned by the powers of the Holy Alliance. In 1827 Russia, Britain, and France, acting alone, not through the congress system, intervened in the conflict on the side of the Greeks and in 1829 obliged Turkey to recognize the independence of Greece.

• The Decembrist Revolt in Russia

In Russia the advocates of liberal reform were forced by censorship and police repression to operate underground. After 1816 many of them joined together in secret societies for the discussion of liberal ideas and possible reforms for the future. The members came largely from among young officers with intellectual interests who had been influenced by their contacts with the West during the Napoleonic Wars. They were, however, inexperienced in politics or in revolution, and they knew little about the life of Russia's peasant masses, even less about the lives of their own soldiers. Not surprisingly they failed when, on December 26, 1825, after the death of Alexander I, they tried to prevent the succession to the throne of Alexander's reactionary brother, Nicholas. The older brother,

Constantine, had privately renounced the succession to the throne, but his action was known only to a very few. Liberal officers tried to induce troops stationed in St. Petersburg to refuse to swear allegiance to Nicholas, but the troops had little interest or understanding of their intended role, and the leaders themselves seemed uncertain as to how to use the troops in a revolutionary situation. Nicholas rallied other troops and readily crushed the revolutionaries. The leaders were tried, some executed, and others exiled to Siberia. It was a naive and futile enterprise yet not without influence in establishing a tradition of struggle against tsarist despotism. It was the last of the palace revolutions in Russia but in its popular orientation was the first *Russian* revolution.

● The French Revolution of 1830

Charles X, who succeeded to the French throne in 1824, ruled in close cooperation with the ultra-royalists and the upper clergy and looked to the largest landowners for his surest political support. He ignored and irritated the growing number of liberal electors and deputies who saw their interests as inseparable from their liberal interpretation of the Charter of 1814 and the preservation of the reforms of the revolution and Napoleon. Charles did not accept the basic principles of the Charter as the opposition understood them and at times at least, seemed to think of himself as a divine right monarch. When his government attempted to establish primogeniture in inheritance, the nation's commitment to equality was offended. When he cut interest on state bonds in order to raise money to indemnify émigrés for property lost during the revolution, he alienated bond holders and bankers. In August 1829 he appointed a ministry headed by Prince Jules de Polignac, a committed reactionary.

When the Chamber of Deputies met for its annual session in March 1830, the deputies heard in Charles' address from the throne an ominous threat to the Charter and to their authority. The deputies voted a reply that openly reproved him by calling on him to dismiss his ministers because they were unacceptable to the majority in the chamber. The King reacted by dissolving the chamber and ordering new elections. He hoped for a majority sympathetic with his own and Polignac's policies, but the election actually increased the representation of the opposition. The short-sighted Charles then concluded that he was confronted with a choice between preservation of royal authority and a republic, and he chose to preserve the former. On July 25 he issued ordinances that censored the press, changed the electoral law to favor conservative candidates, dissolved the newly-chosen chamber, and ordered new elections. The ordinances sparked a revolution in Paris. After three days of street fighting royal troops were forced from the capital, and on August 2 Charles abdicated. A handful of opposition deputies offered the crown to Louis-Philippe, the Duke of Orleans, and on August 9 he formally accepted it. The Parisian crowd, aided by liberal journalists and deputies, had driven a legitimate monarch from his throne, an open defiance of the settlement of 1815. But the revolution in Paris was over quickly, and it had stopped short of a republic. Louis-Philippe was a member of the Bourbon family, and the nation was still a monarchy. The conservative European monarchs reluctantly recognized the new regime.

• Revolt in Belgium, 1830

Another and, as it developed, more serious threat to the international order, came from Belgium, where revolution, inspired by the recent French example, broke out on August 25, 1830.

The Belgians over the centuries had been fairly amenable subjects under many regimes, but King William of the Netherlands, who added them to his country in 1815, pursued policies that soon drove them to rebellion. They complained of inadequate representation in the national assembly, of public offices filled largely by Dutchmen, of discriminatory taxation, and of a tariff system that benefitted Dutch trade but failed to protect Belgian manufacturers. They resented having their capital city in Holland. As Catholics they were offended by the religious equality prescribed by the Protestant Dutch. The designation of Dutch as the official language in all except French-speaking areas appeared to the Belgians as an attempt to turn them into Dutchmen. In 1830 the country was ripe for rebellion.

At first the Belgians sought only self-government within the Kingdom of the Netherlands, but when King William tried to suppress the revolt by force and failed, Belgian leaders proclaimed their country's independence and set up a provisional government. A constituent assembly drafted a constitution and summoned Prince Leopold of Saxe-Coburg to become the first king of the Belgians. William appealed to the great powers for help. Not only did Britain and France refuse aid and deter the other powers from sending help, but France with British agreement twice despatched a French army into Belgium to oppose Dutch repressive measures, and the British sent war vessels to restrain the Dutch. The two liberal powers supported a revolt against a legitimate monarch, and simultaneous troubles in Poland and Italy contributed to restraining inclinations to intervene that the conservative monarchies might have had.

In 1840 the major powers agreed that Belgium should be an independent country and guaranteed its perpetual neutrality, the latter being thought of at the time as a safeguard against renewed French aggression. The outcome was, however, another break in the settlement of 1815.

• Revolt in Poland

While the Belgian Revolution was still unresolved, the Poles in November 1830 rose in revolt against their Russian overlords. Leadership came from the aristocracy, army officers, and students. Even urban workers supported the movement, but the mass of the population, composed of peasants, was not directly involved. The Polish Diet deposed Tsar Nicholas as King of Poland, and the provisional government sought help from abroad, but in vain. Even the new Orleanist regime in France, itself a product of revolution, declined to send aid. Nicholas, fearful and distrustful of revolutionaries, rejected offers of negotiation from the rebel leaders. The Polish forces won some minor engagements, but once the Russian troops arrived in force the issue was quickly decided. In the autumn of 1831 Nicholas put the country under martial law and executed or exiled many Polish leaders. Poland lost the small measure of independence that the Congress of Vienna had given it and was incorporated into Russia, and the Russian government took severe repressive measures to extinguish the remaining embers of Polish nationalism.

• Revolt in Italy

Metternich found his most vexing problems in Italy. Sporadic nationalist disturbances had occurred throughout the twenties. The Carbonari and other liberal secret societies were plotting a coordinated revolt throughout the peninsula. Guiseppi Mazzini, founder of the Young Italy Movement, which was working for a united and republican Italy was the leading figure, though some nationalists looked to Duke Francis of Modena for leadership. In February 1831 revolts looking to the exclusion of Austria from northern Italy broke out in Parma, Modena, and the Papal States. The leaders expected aid from the French, but Louis-Philippe refused it, and that led to Duke of Francis of Modena to withhold his support. The Austrians readily suppressed the revolt, and Metternich was confirmed in his view that the great powers must intervene in other states to prevent the spread of revolutionary contagion. The events of 1830-31 had threatened the conservative principles of the Vienna settlement, but conservative regimes still ruled central and eastern Europe. Revolution had been contained everywhere save in Belgium and France, and even there the worst — a republic — had been avoided. Most of the old order remained.

17

The Problems of Progress

IN THE MIDDLE THIRD of the nineteenth century industrial growth accelerated rapidly in Europe. The earlier industrial revolution in Britain and Belgium was more than matched by enormous growth in other parts of Europe. Heavy industry began to emerge in the Ruhr Valley of western Germany, in central France, and in northern Italy. A progressively affluent middle class grew with the industrial economy, and the grimy factory town with uniform slum dwellings row upon row became an inseparable part of the European landscape. Railroad networks spread over western and central Europe and began to move raw materials and finished products with unheard of speed and economy. Consumers had an exploding richness of goods to purchase. At the same time the railroads gave Europeans unprecedented mobility, carried urban influences into rural hinterlands, and brought to central governments new powers of coercion over their citizens and subjects. Free trade became gospel in Britain. Early socialists, moved by their observations of the deficiencies and abuses of capitalist free enterprise, developed theories and prescriptions for the social control of the means of production. Nationalism triumphed in the unification of two great national states, Germany and Italy.

• Tory Reform in Britain

On the Continent autocracy and repression forced advocates of change to turn to violence, but in Britain the parliamentary system permitted change to come by peaceful means. Many of the same political and social pressures for change existed there, and in the 1820s the Tories, led by George Canning, Robert Peel, and William Huskisson, responded to it with a number of laws that began an era of reform continuing into the 1840s. Changes in the criminal code and reductions in tariffs have been mentioned earlier. In 1826 a poor harvest prompted the relaxation of the Corn Law of 1815, the first legislative expression of a movement that would culminate in the total repeal of the Corn Laws in 1846.

The Duke of Wellington, who succeeded to the leadership of the Tories in 1827 and appeared more conservative than his predecessor, did however initiate reforms, one of the most controversial of which was the political emancipation of British Catholics. The Test Act of 1673, still in force, required that all officeholders be communicants of the Church of England. The act served to exclude Catholics from office, but many non-Anglican Protestants had held office only by evasion of its provisions. In 1828 Parliament ended the application of the law to non-Anglican Protestants, but the granting of equal rights to Catholics was more difficult because it was embroiled in the complex and emotionally charged Irish question. In 1828 an Irish Catholic leader, Daniel O'Connell, ran for a seat in Parliament, knowing that his religion would prevent his taking the oaths of allegiance and supremacy required by the Test Act and that consequently he would be barred from the House of Commons. He was elected, and Wellington, fearing that refusing him his seat on these grounds might set off civil war in Ireland, pushed through parliament the Catholic Emancipation Bill of 1829, which opened parliament and all but two public offices to Catholics. Irish nationalists were emboldened by the results of their defiance, and now that Catholics would be sitting in Parliament Irish grievances and protests were sure to be more frequently heard and Irish demands more vigorously pushed.

By 1830 the spirit of reform had spread to include the reform of Parliament itself. The franchise in many boroughs was so severely limited that aristocratic patrons chose members from the "pocket" or "rotten" constituencies with no regard for the welfare of the people living there. No changes in parliamentary districts had been made since the seventeenth century, so that in some instances almost completely depopulated boroughs were represented in Parliament while new industrial cities such as Leeds and Manchester had almost no voice. The Whigs saw parliamentary reform as a good issue to ride back into power. Between 1830 and 1832, when revolution shook many European countries, Britain, too, had its

Street fighting in Paris, June 1848. Courtesy, Cabinet des Estamples, Bibliothèque nationale, Paris.

share of political violence. Electoral campaigns involving the heated issue of parliamentary reform set off riots in many districts, and there were fears that England might follow in the paths of her continental neighbors. The Whig Earl Grey became prime minister in 1830 and introduced a bill to reform parliamentary representation. The Tories fought it and for a time succeeded in blocking the bill in the House of Lords. After a new election and extraordinary pressure from the crown, including the threat to pack the House of Lords by the creation of new peers, both houses passed the bill. It redistributed seats, giving cities and towns fairer representation, and nearly doubled the size of the electorate. The Reform Act of 1832 was an important breakthrough. Its passage soon meant that the landed aristocracy had to share more of the governing power with the new urban industrial elite, and in the long run it opened the way to further parliamentary reform in which a more democratic House of Commons began to assume legislative and governmental ascendancy in Britain.

In the next two decades both Whigs and Tories were active reformers, each party attacking the abuses and privileges that benefited the other. In 1833 Parliament abolished slavery throughout the British Empire. In 1835 the Municipal Corporations Act ended the traditional oligarchic rule of British cities and provided for government both more democratic and more effective in dealing with newly emerging problems. The Factory Act of 1833, the Mine Act of 1842, and the Ten Hour Act of 1847 limited the hours of work by women and children in factories and mines and in practice imposed the same limits on the hours of men, since varying hours by age or sex was impractical. In 1834 a new Poor Law substituted a more humane method of poor relief for the system inherited from the seventeenth century.

• France under Louis-Philippe

Across the channel France was being ruled by a king and a parliament that represented chiefly large landed interests. The electoral law of 1831, a product of the Revolution of 1830, had doubled the electorate, but high tax qualifications still limited the vote to about three per cent of the male adults. The smallness of the electorate made it easy for the government to exert pressure on electors, and elections were often corrupted by both the government and the opposition.

The first four years of the Orleanist regime were insecure and marked by recurring violence. Bloody street riots bordering on insurrection occurred in Lyon in 1831 and 1834 and in Paris in 1832 and 1834. Many attempts were made on the king's life. But after 1834 the economy revived, the republican movement was broken up, revolutionary violence largely disappeared, and France entered upon a period of extraordinary modernization. Construction of railroads began in earnest, the network of hard-surfaced roads was extended, and the electrical telegraph introduced. The expansion of the cotton textile and heavy metals industries mark these years as the beginning of France's industrial revolution. Population began to shift out of poorer rural areas and into developing urban centers. The School Law of 1833 required every commune to have a primary school, and by the 1840s its influence was evident in rising literacy rates.

• The First Socialists

Industrial and urban growth brought a new concern for and a fear of the urban working class, and the 1830s and 1840s were years rich in discussion of how poverty might be prevented or attenuated. The Saint-Simonians, followers of the Count Henri de Saint-Simon (1760-1825), a nobleman turned philosopher and economist, tried to adapt the optimistic rationalism of the Enlightenment to the problems of a nascent industrial society. They advocated direction of the economy by engineers, scientists, businessmen, and bankers, who would maximize production and organize distribution to benefit the "poorest and most numerous class." The state would become the sole heir, ending privately inherited wealth, and, through the banks, redistribute it in the interest of stimulating production. Saint Simonianism influenced later socialists, who took over its ideas on central economic planning and direction and the abolition of private inheritance. Through its ideas on state intervention to stimulate the economy and on the key role of banking it inspired many of the entrepreneurs of the latter half of the century.

Charles Fourier (1772-1837) proposed an appealing plan to replace competition, which he felt led to exploitation and poverty, with cooperation or association. Maintaining that human desires were so distributed that if the correct number of persons were organized into a producers' cooperative and allowed to follow their own desires, all work would be done efficiently and happily, he proposed the organization of communities, called *phalanges*, of 1624 members each who would share equally in production, direction, and the communities' products. Fourier believed that the *phalanges* would be so productive and so socially beneficial that they would spread to all branches of the economy and eventually replace all private enterprise.

Fourier's basic idea of cooperative communities was popularized by a Parisian journalist, Louis Blanc. *The Organization of Labor*, published in 1840, presented in brief and readable form a plan for the establishment of "social workshops" and "social farms", producer cooperatives like Fourier's *phalanges*, that would eventually embrace the whole economy and replace competition with association. In the 1840s Blanc's phrases and ideas became part of the revolutionary vocabulary and program of the militant Parisian working class, and in 1848 it would demand that the new republican government apply them in practice. Across the English Channel the exiled Louis-Napoleon, the future Napoleon III, published in 1844 a pamphlet, *The Extinction of Pauperism,* clearly inspired by Louis Blanc's earlier pamphlet. It associated reviving Bonapartism with the demand for social reform.

Paris in the 1840s was the world's fount of revolutionary social ideas, and here modern socialism was formed. In Paris in this seminal decade, in addition to the Saint-Simonians, the Fourierists, and Louis Blanc, were Pierre Joseph Proudhon, Karl Marx, and many others. Proudhon is remembered especially for his attack on private property indelibly proclaimed in his sentence, "Property is theft," but he is important also for his advocacy of social revolution that would guarantee personal liberty as well as equality. Karl Marx lived in Paris in 1843-44 and here acquired and formulated his concept of the proletariat as the revolutionary class.

The Catholic church in France was essentially conservative, but many Catholics were disturbed by the same inequities and injustices that moved the early socialists. One of them, a young priest named Félicité Lamennais, published in 1834, *The Words of a Believer,* a book that shook the Catholic world by its preaching of a gospel of social insurrection to win for the masses a share in government and in the growing national wealth. The church disavowed Lamennais, but the book sold by the hundreds of thousands and liberal Catholicism continued as a force for reform in France.

• French Foreign Policy

In foreign relations Louis-Philippe and the wealthy propertied class that supported him at home were committed to peace, not because they were morally or even economically opposed to war but because their experience led them to associate war with revolution, and they feared revolution. In 1830-32 Louis-Philippe, in cooperation with Britain, supported the Belgians in their successful battle for independence and then tried to form an alliance with Britain as a safeguard against the hostility of the conservative monarchies to the east. The latter effort failed, and in 1840 France came close to war with a revived anti-French coalition, including Britain, over conflict of interests in the eastern Mediterranean.

LE VENTRE LÉGISLATIF.

The French Legislature in the 1840's as portrayed by Honoré Daumier. Courtesy, Museum of Fine Arts, Boston.

Louis-Philippe, however, backed away from war, and in the succeeding years revived the entente with Britain. When that policy fell victim to a dispute over the succession to the Spanish throne, he moved close to conservative Austria. Republicans and Bonapartists charged the regime with betraying France's glorious past, but the Orleanist policy was agreeable to the conservatives who dominated government and parliament. In 1846-47, however, an old-style agrarian crisis stemming from poor harvests combined with an industrial depression to spread distress among the poor and to shake the faith of the elite in the ability of the Orleanist regime to govern effectively.

● Conservative Central and Eastern Europe

Central and eastern Europe continued to be dominated by ultra-conservative monarchies. In Austria the bureaucracy and the police kept the population well quarantined against dangerous outside ideas. In Prussia repression was much lighter, but neither king nor bureaucracy was sympathetic with liberalism; the *Zollverein* was the only significant liberal innovation before 1848.

In Russia Tsar Nicholas I feared the ideas and example of the French Revolution and based his regime on the concepts of Orthodoxy, autocracy, and nationality. Personally he was deeply religious, and he sought to impose religious uniformity on his subjects. He believed in and practiced divine right monarchy and organized a political police, known as the "Third Section," to seek out and destroy any deviation from officially-approved views. As a committed Russian nationalist he sought to Russify subject nationalities such as the Poles and to wipe out all vestiges of their national cultures. Nicholas did recognize serfdom as "the indubitable evil of Russian life" and appointed several commissions to study ways of freeing the serfs and state peasants, who made up some 80 percent of the Russian population, but nothing further was accomplished during his reign.

In the 1830s and 1840s there emerged two influential literary and philosophical groups that probed the Russian character and the nature of Russia's historical development. The Westerners believed that Russia was part of western European civilization and that it must follow the West's pattern of development. Its obvious differences from the West were simply the result of slower development, and the nation should exert itself to catch up, following the lead of the more advanced countries of the West. The Slavophils emphasized the uniqueness of Russian civilization. Russia was fundamentally different from the West, and it should continue to pursue its own distinctive development and not try to copy the now decadent West. These contrasting views would have significant influence in shaping not only literary tastes but political and social beliefs and programs as well.

• The Revolution of 1848 in France

The great year of revolution in nineteenth-century Europe was 1848. To contemporaries it seemed that liberalism and nationalism, held in check but not extinguished since 1815, were about to triumph over conservatism and legitimacy. As had happened earlier, the conflagration first broke out in France.

Economic depression, scandals involving persons in high place, and the government's rigid opposition to extension of the very limited franchise undermined public confidence in the regime of Louis-Philippe and encouraged its enemies to bolder action. On February 22, 1848, the government's banning of an opposition political rally in Paris led to street demonstrations, which on February 24 turned into insurrection. Most of the National Guard, until then regarded as a bulwark of the regime, defected, and the army alone could not control the city or defend the royal palace. Louis-Philippe abdicated, and republicans moved into the vacuum. They proclaimed the Second Republic, established a provisional government, and ordered the election by universal manhood suffrage of a national assembly to give France a new constitution.

The victorious republicans were seriously divided, and the history of the French Revolution of 1848 from February to June is the history of a struggle for power between the moderate republicans, who wanted only a political revolution, and the radical social republicans, who wanted both a political revolution and a social revolution. Under pressure from the latter and their working class supporters in Paris who manned the barricades and filled the streets with demonstrators, the moderate provisional government effected in its first few days in power a modest social revolution. It proclaimed the right to work as a new natural right of man and established National Workshops, suggestive in name of Louis Blanc's social workshops, to guarantee that right. They limited the hours of work of all workers, not only women and children, to ten hours daily in Paris, eleven hours in the provinces. They authorized Louis Blanc to organize the Luxembourg Commission, a kind of labor parliament, to discuss and recommend reforms in the economy.

In succeeding weeks the moderates recovered their courage. The government organized a new anti-riot force, the *Garde mobile,* and the sympathies of the National Guard shifted to the moderate side. Elections in April returned a majority of moderate and conservative republicans to the Constituent Assembly. Meanwhile the National Workshops in Paris had grown to enormous size, as the unemployed flocked into the capital in search of work. There was not enough work for all, and thousands were simply maintained in idleness on a minimum dole. Conservatives in the assembly feared the workshops as a threat of imminent revolution and moved quickly to disband them. Republican militants, workshop men, and just simple, embittered, and poverty-stricken workers reacted violently to this decision. For four days, June 23-26, Paris experienced the most bitter and savage street fighting of its history. It ended in victory for the forces of order in the dissolution of the workshops and in the triumph of the conservative republicans.

The assembly returned to constitution-making. Its new instrument was adopted in November 1848 and presidential elections held in December. A few weeks earlier Louis-Napoleon Bonaparte, nephew of Napoleon I, had won election to the assembly and returned to France from his long exile. He soon announced his candidacy for the presidency of the republic. Although his opponents were well-known political figures and he was little known, the magic of his name and the popular will for law and order after a tumultuous year of revolution won him three times as many votes as all his competitors combined. On December 20, 1848, he took the oath of office as President of the Republic.

The establishment of the republic in Paris in February 1848, aroused fears throughout conservative Europe that France would again as in 1792-1814 become the aggressive, crusading nation carrying republican ideas and institutions into the territories of her neighbors. The dominant republican leaders, however, had no desire to imperil their new and uncertain position at home by engaging in foreign adventures, and the ministry assured the powers of the republic's peaceful intentions. On the other hand, the government could not control the influence of France's example, and it set off revolutions throughout central Europe.

• The Revolution of 1848 in Germany

In Germany and Italy the revolutions of 1848 were both liberal and nationalist, directed at winning both constitutional government and national unification. Since 1815 Germany had been a loose confederation of thirty-nine sovereign states dominated by their largest peers, Austria and Prussia. In May 1848 a popularly elected German parliament, known as the Frankfurt National Assembly, met in Frankfurt for the purpose of drawing up a constitution for a united German nation-state. While the power of Austria and Prussia was in eclipse owing to revolutions in Vienna and Berlin, the Frankfort Assembly acted like a German national government, but it was internally divided over the question of what lands to include in united Germany, and it never acquired an armed force of its own. Once the Austrian and Prussian governments had mastered their own revolutionaries and recovered their military capabilities, the assembly became a charade. In the spring of 1849 it elected Frederick William IV of Prussia Emperor of Germany. He spurned the offer, saying that he would not pick up a crown from the gutter. A few weeks later Prussian troops dispersed the rump of the assembly, putting an emphatic end to the attempt to unite Germany by parliamentary means. It would be achieved later by "iron and blood."

In Berlin a revolution beginning in mid-March 1848 forced Frederick William to convene a Prussian constituent assembly, to promise support of the movement for German national unification, and eventually to abandon his capital. The revolutionaries sought to break the dominance over Prussia of the Junkers, the large landowners, but their efforts ended when Frederick William ordered his army back into Berlin and dissolved the assembly. He did grant his subjects a constitution, nominally a victory for liberalism, but it provided for a system of class voting that assured control of the parliament by the large landed interests and left the crown's executive powers virtually untouched. Frederick William's constitution remained the public law of Prussia until 1918.

● The Revolution of 1848 in Austria

The Austrian Empire, although ruled by Germans, was composed of many nationalities, and among all the subject nationalities the French Revolution and Napoleon had planted liberal and nationalist ideas. The government in Vienna had worked diligently since 1815 to wipe them out and to silence those who advocated them. But in March 1848 the winds from Paris fanned the smoldering grievances of nationalists and liberals into revolution. Within a few weeks revolutions broke out in Vienna, Milan, Venice, and Prague. In Budapest the Hungarians demanded self-government, the Croats demanded autonomy, and a Pan-Slav Congress met in Prague and proclaimed the solidarity of all Slavic peoples against the Germans.

The revolution in Vienna forced the resignation and flight of Metternich, the abolition of repressive measures against liberals, and the calling of a constituent assembly. The emperor himself had to flee his own capital, but in June the tide began to turn. Austrian armies moved from city to city suppressing revolutions with much bloodshed and frequent brutality. In Budapest the Austrians were assisted by 100,000 Russian troops supplied by Tsar Nicholas I, who was apprehensive of the revolutionary tide approaching his lands. By 1850 the Habsburg Empire was again made safe for autocracy, and bureaucratic rule from Vienna was restored.

● The Revolution of 1848 in Italy

In March 1848 Italian nationalists seized control of Milan and Venice, capitals of the Habsburg provinces of Lombardy and Venetia. The Kingdom of Piedmont, the leading independent north Italian state, came to their assistance and so too did some forces from central and southern Italy. Early the next year revolutionaries in the Papal States in effect deposed the Pope as a temporal ruler and proclaimed the Roman Republic. But nationalist and liberal enthusiasm proved to be no match for the Austrian armies. In 1849 General Joseph Radetsky crushed the revolutions.

By 1851 the European Revolutions of 1848, save in France, had come full circle. Everywhere conservatives were again firmly entrenched. Germany remained divided under the revived Confederation of 1815. The

Austrian Germans ruled their subject nationalities from Vienna. A united Italy was still only a dream. The defeat of nationalists and liberals was owing in part to their lack of armed forces to match those of the military monarchies but also to the absence in still largely peasant central Europe of a large revolutionary class, either bourgeois or proletarian.

• Victorian Britain in Mid-Century

The middle third of the nineteenth century in Britain saw the beginning of the Victorian Age. Queen Victoria came to the throne in 1837, and in her reign, which continued until 1903, Great Britain achieved the pinnacle of her power and wealth. In 1840 Victoria married Prince Albert of Saxe-Coburg-Gotha, to whom she became devoted, and he – in the office of royal private secretary as well as Prince Consort – became virtual joint-ruler of Britain until his untimely death in 1861.

In the first decade of Victoria's reign probably the most significant single achievement of the government was the repeal of the Corn Laws in 1846 which abolished all tariffs on imports of food. This act was followed in the next several years by the elimination of all protective tariffs. The shift to free trade had a double significance: it proclaimed that British industry enjoyed such predominance in world markets that it need fear no competition, and it affirmed the growing ascendancy of industrial interests over agrarian interests in the determination of public policy.

Britain was not untouched by the reformist and revolutionary effervescence of the late 1840s. The latter found expression most conspicuously in the Chartist movement, a working class movement that proclaimed its demands in a petition or charter. It called for the democratization of British government by the establishment of universal manhood suffrage, vote by secret ballot (to protect freedom of choice), the elimination of property qualifications for members of Parliament, and pay for members (who then served without pay). Parliament refused to act on the petition in 1838 and again in 1842. In 1848 the revolution in Paris revived the movement – some two million people signed a new petition, and militants among them threatened violence in support of their demands. The government mobilized imposing repressive forces, and the danger passed without either violence or the granting of any of the Chartists' demands. Before the century was out, however, all had been achieved by peaceful means.

• France under Napoleon III

As President of the Republic Louis-Napoleon soon became embroiled in conflict with the monarchist and conservative republican majority in the National Assembly. He was anxious to prolong his term of office beyond the prescribed three years, and when the assembly refused its consent, he seized power in a coup d'état on December 2, 1851, the anniversary of the first Napoleon's great victory at Austerlitz in 1805. He justified his action as necessary to save France from radical republican revolution, and a huge majority of citizens, voting in a plebiscite, approved his action. He granted a constitution that preserved the forms of democratic and parliamentary government but vested full powers in himself as president for ten years. A year later he reestablished the empire and took the title of Napoleon III, Emperor of the French.

The Second Empire was a period of renewed — and in its first decade rapid — economic growth. Some 8,700 miles of railroad lines were built with government aid, and by the end of the empire in 1870 the main lines of the national network were complete. Railroad construction gave a powerful stimulus to the iron, steel, and timber industries. The cotton textile industry flourished until slowed by the shortage of raw cotton during the American Civil War. The building industry prospered from the government's lavish public works programs which included the rebuilding of Paris, the first great reconstruction of an old and established city in modern times. In two decades Napoleon III and his Prefect of the Seine, Baron Georges Haussmann, converted Paris from a congested, overgrown, almost medieval town to the city of broad avenues and spacious parks familiar to the twentieth-century visitor. The execution of public works and industrial expansion were facilitated by the establishment of new and innovative banking institutions capable of making long-term investments, such as the *Credit foncier* and the *Credit mobilier*, whose founders were influenced by Saint-Simonian ideas picked up in their youth. The first deposit banks, established in the 1860s, pioneered in retail banking. Large department stores began to shape both retail trade practices and popular tastes. Trade treaties negotiated first with England in 1860 and then with a dozen other countries brought France close to free trade and exposed French industry to salutary competition.

In the 1850s Napoleon ruled as a virtual dictator, but beginning in 1860 he voluntarily relaxed his regime, and by 1870 the so-called Liberal Empire had most of the attributes of a parliamentary regime with the sovereign power vested in the popularly-elected Legislative Body. Napoleon's most significant political accomplishment, however, was his demonstration to a skeptical world that universal manhood suffrage could be combined with a stable, even a conservative regime, a lesson that Bismarck followed when he established the German Empire. Yet Napoleon failed to hold the support of the many constituencies that had backed him in 1848 and 1851. His foreign and religious policies alienated Catholics.

His tariff policy alienated industrialists. Many true Bonapartists deplored his liberalization of the empire, and, on the other hand, the liberalization failed to disarm the republican opposition. The defeat in the war with Prussia in 1870 revealed how fragile the empire had become.

- ## War in the Crimea

The turmoil of 1848-49 had scarcely subsided when a new crisis arose over the Eastern Question, which had brought Europe close to war in 1840. For centuries the French and the Russians had served as spokesmen to the Turks for Catholic and Orthodox Christians in the Ottoman Empire. Their actions were usually directed at assuring protection and privileges for pilgrims to Christian holy places in Palestine. Napoleon III issued a vigorous restatement of French rights, and Tsar Nicholas followed his example, the two rulers making conflicting demands on the Sultan. Britain's economic interests and her anxiety not to upset the balance of power in the eastern Mediterranean brought her into the dispute in support of France. Both sides made shows of force. An Anglo-French fleet passed through the Dardanelles, violating the international Straits Convention of 1841, and the Russians occupied the Ottoman provinces of Moldavia and Wallachia. In October 1853 Turkey declared war on Russia, and the next spring the British and the French joined Turkey in the war, claiming to be protecting the integrity of the Ottoman Empire.

The war has gone down in history as a classical example of military incompetence. The charge of the English Light Cavalry Brigade at Balaclava demonstrated great courage but abysmal leadership. Florence Nightingale's nursing revealed the appalling state of medical services in the British army. On the other side Russian direction of the war was so shockingly disastrous that even the tsar and his conservative advisers agreed that the system must be drastically reformed. After the war's end in 1855 with Russia's defeat, the powers gathered in Paris to make the peace. There they agreed to ban Russian and Turkish war vessels from the Black Sea and again closed the straits between the Mediterranean and the Black Sea to warships of all nations.

Austria had remained neutral in the war, irritating the Russians, who, recalling their aid to Austria against the rebellious Hungarians in 1849, expected assistance in their time of need. The Kingdom of Sardinia (Piedmont) had joined the western allies in the war in hope of being rewarded by help in driving the Austrians out of Italy, but no help was forthcoming at this time. Napoleon III and the French were the principal beneficiaries of the war. The French army demonstrated its superiority. Russia had been humbled, and Napoleon could claim that he had broken

Surrender of Napoleon III to King William of Prussia, 1870.

the system of 1815 that had been imposed by France's enemies after the fall of the first Napoleon.

• The Great Reforms in Russia

The reign of Alexander II of Russia (1855-81) stands out from all the others of nineteenth-century Russia as the great age of reform. Alexander came to the throne amid the failures and defeats of the Crimean War which had discredited the military and the bureaucracy and stirred widespread demands for reform. The greatest evil of the old order, most agreed, was serfdom. It was a moral blight, no longer profitable to most landowners, and many feared that its continuation would sooner or later produce a general peasant revolt.

Once the war was ended, Alexander's government had provincial committees of nobles set up throughout Russia to discuss methods of emancipating the serfs. From them came many proposals, but in the end the Emancipation Edict and Statutes of 1861 were largely the work of a few enlightened civil servants in St. Petersburg. The edict and statutes gave the serfs personal freedom and a share of the land they had cultivated. Ownership of peasant land, however, was vested not in individual peasants but in peasant communes or *mirs*. The government paid landlords for land transferred to the *mirs* and undertook to recover the payments from the *mirs* over a period of forty-nine years. No peasant might leave his commune until he had paid his share, so that although the peasant was legally free, he remained bound to the *mir* by financial obligations. Moreover, the redemption payments were heavy and the land over-populated. Serfdom was gone, but poverty and oppression remained, and so too did peasant resentment and anger.

The Russian judicial system was reorganized on the English model. Courts were made independent of the administration, and trials made public with legally trained judges secure in office. The law code was Westernized, all subjects became equal before the law, and jurisdiction over minor crimes was taken from landlords. Trial by jury was instituted and rights of the accused safeguarded. Reforms in the army in 1874 made military service less onerous: the term of service was cut from twenty-five years to six and all classes became equally liable for service, the more barbarous military punishments were eliminated, and the training of officers improved. The army instituted a program of education among conscripts, and many peasants learned to read and write — and even picked up some revolutionary ideas — during their military service.

Alexander established regional assemblies (*zemstvos*) composed of representatives of nobles, peasants, and townspeople to deal with local problems such as road building, education, food supply, and health care. They functioned reasonably well and gave all participants some experience in self-government, a rare quality in autocratic Russia. Taxpayers in towns were permitted to elect municipal councils with some authority in the management of local affairs. The first steps were taken to provide primary education for all. Restoration of freedom to universities and relaxation of censorship permitted the influx and circulation of new ideas from western Europe, including the new socialist ideas from France and Germany.

The Great Reforms, and the process of industrialization which began soon after, contributed to the democratization of Russian society and the modernization of the economy, but the central government remained autocratic, and all change came slowly and erratically and with much back sliding. Many Russians, especially the intellectuals, were impatient, and in the 1860s a Russian revolutionary movement began to take shape. From beginnings in nihilism, a moral rebellion against all established institutions and all obligation imposed upon the individual, the revolutionary current moved through a frustrating attempt to win the peasantry over to socialism and an equally unsuccessful effort to convert urban workers into street fighters, to terrorism directed against key figures in the government. Terrorism, the revolutionaries concluded, was the only form of effective political action possible in a police state. On March 13, 1881, terrorists "executed" the tsar himself and brought down upon Russia renewed reaction and heavy repression.

The Unification of Italy

Since his early youth Louis-Napoleon had had a sentimental attachment to the cause of Italian liberation, and as emperor he had proclaimed himself a friend of nationalities and made vague commitments to aid Italian nationalists. In January 1858 an exasperated Italian nationalist attempted to assassinate him, reminding him of his personal involvement in the Italian national cause. In July 1858 he met Camille Cavour, the Prime Minister of Sardinia, at Plombières in eastern France, and there Napoleon agreed to provide military aid in a war to drive the Austrians from northern Italy. Cavour provoked the Austrians to war the next spring, and Napoleon, following in his uncle's footsteps, personally led his armies into Italy.

After two bloody victories at Magenta on June 4 and at Solferino on June 24, Napoleon, without consulting Cavour, met with Emperor Franz Joseph of Austria and arranged an armistice before the whole of northern Italy had been liberated. A wave of nationalist revolts spread across the peninsula, and Guiseppe Garibaldi and his band of Red Shirts conquered Sicily and most of southern Italy. The liberated territories voted to join Sardinia, and on March 17, 1861, the new united Kingdom of Italy was formally proclaimed. On the whole peninsula only Venetia and Rome remained outside the new nation. Venetia would be added in 1866, Rome in 1870. For his efforts Napoleon acquired Nice and Savoy. He also acquired a new, united, and possibly dangerous neighbor on his southeastern frontier.

France's Mexican Expedition

The Italian War had unfortunate consequences for Napoleon III. Catholics blamed him for the diminution of Papal power and influence. His aiding in the creation of a potentially dangerous neighbor caused French nationalists to question his competence to defend France's national interests. His decision to intervene in Mexico in support of a

Catholic monarch against a popular revolution was undertaken in part to win back Catholic allegiance at home. The first move into Mexico in 1862 was a joint venture with Britain and Spain to secure the payment of Mexican debts to foreign creditors, but when the allies withdrew, the French not only remained but directed their efforts toward establishing a Mexican Empire with the Austrian Archduke Maximilian as emperor. The choice of Maximilian, too, was in part an effort to repair an ill effect of the Italian War, the break with Austria. By 1863 Napoleon had committed 30,000 men to the expedition. In 1864 an assembly of Mexican conservatives, meeting under French protection, offered the crown to Maximilian. He accepted and came to Mexico and assumed the office, but his regime, imposed from above, had no popular support and existed only under French protection. With the end of the Civil War in 1865 the United States government was again able to enforce the Monroe Doctrine, and it demanded the withdrawal of the French forces. About the same time Prussia's resounding victory over Austria raised a new threat on France's eastern frontier, and Napoleon needed all his troops at home. The last French soldiers left Mexico early in 1867. Five months later Maximilian, his empire fallen before republican attack, was brought before a firing squad and shot. The Mexican expedition had brought to France only losses in men and money and to Napoleon only a further erosion of his prestige.

● Bismarck and the Unification of Northern Germany

While Napoleon's domestic and Mexican problems grew, ominous clouds were gathering across the Rhine. In 1862 Otto von Bismarck became Minister President of Prussia and set the country on an aggressive path. He was a Junker and had no sympathy with the liberal aspirations of 1848. Napoleon III's intervention in the war in Italy in 1859 had raised the spectre of renewed French aggression on the Rhine, and the Regent, the future King William I, appointed a new war minister to enlarge and to improve the Prussian army. In 1860 the ministry asked the *Landtag* for credits for this purpose, but liberals blocked the appropriation. The frustrated King William considered abdicating but was persuaded to call Bismarck from his post as Prussian ambassador in Paris to head the ministry. As minister president Bismarck defied the *Landtag,* collected the necessary taxes, and carried out the army reforms.

By 1864 the new, reformed army was ready to be tested in the field. Toward the end of 1863 a dynastic and constitutional dispute had arisen over the attempt of Denmark to annex Schleswig, which had a large German population. The Diet of the Germanic Confederation decided on an all-German war to save Schleswig for Germany; Bismarck, who had no desire to strengthen the confederation, chose to follow an independent policy and coerced Austria into joining him. The Prussian army, with limited support from Austria, invaded Schleswig and defeated the Danes, and Prussian troops remained in occupation of the province.

In 1865 Bismarck talked with Napoleon III at his summer residence at Biarritz to sound out his attitude toward a Prussian war to force Austria out of Germany. Napoleon was sympathetic with the cause of German national unity and with the idea of Prussia's leading the move to unification, and Bismarck came away from the meeting encouraged to move ahead with his plans. Napoleon prepared for the impending showdown in Germany by obtaining commitments from Prussia and Austria to make no territorial changes in Germany without consulting France and to permit Italy, pledged to join Prussia in war against Austria, to annex Venetia. Whichever way the war should go Napoleon expected to play a key role in making the peace.

The Prussian army quickly and decisively defeated the Austrians in the so-called Seven Weeks War, the decisive battle being won on July 3, 1866, at Sadowa (or Königgrätz) in Bohemia. By that overwhelming victory Prussia became the dominant power in Germany, and Austria was excluded, just as six years earlier she had been excluded from her formerly dominant role in Italy. Napoleon's expectations of being able to shape the final settlement were quickly dashed; the crucial decisions were made by Bismarck and made quickly. French nationalists faulted the emperor for his failure to win compensations for France to balance the increase in Prussian power. He had decided against mobilization of French forces on the Rhine when a show of force might have made a difference, and when he belatedly made proposals to Bismarck for territorial compensations in Luxembourg or Belgium, Bismarck at first encouraged him, then turned him down in a way that discredited him in the eyes of Europe as an inept but dangerous expansionist.

Under Bismarck's leadership the German states north of the Main River joined with Prussia in the North German Confederation with the King of Prussia as the president. The old Germanic Confederation, formed in 1815 and dominated by Austria and Prussia jointly, ceased to exist. Austria, excluded from both Germany and Italy, turned her imperial ambitions toward the Balkans.

In preparation for this new role, the Austrian Germans reached an agreement with the Magyars of Hungary, the Compromise of 1867, which created the Dual Monarchy of Austria-Hungary, two states joined in personal union of a common monarchy and three joint ministries. The rule of the many subject nationalities of the empire was divided between the Austrians and the Magyars, an arrangement that satisfied only the two principals. Nationalist resentments against them and the threat of nationalist revolts remained.

• Prussian Unification of All Germany

Bismarck's next goal in Germany was to bring the four south German states into the North German Confederation. Since they were reluctant to join, Bismarck concluded that fear of France might force them in. He, therefore, undertook to provoke Napoleon III into war on Germany, and he found his opportunity in the problem of the succession to the throne of Spain. In 1868 a revolution had deposed Queen Isabella, and the constituent assembly eventually offered the crown to Prince Leopold of Hohenzollern-Sigmaringen, a cousin of the King of Prussia. Leopold accepted. When the French government learned of this, it protested strongly, and Leopold withdrew his candidacy. The French ministry then ineptly sought additional assurances, hoping for a resounding diplomatic victory to compensate for the reserves of 1866-67, and Bismarck maneuvered them into a position where they had either to go to war or accept a stinging diplomatic rebuff. The tenuous political situation of the empire at home made the former course appear the less dangerous, and on July 19, 1870, the French government declared war on Prussia.

As Bismarck had hoped, the south German states joined with those of the north, and under the command of the Prussian General Staff the combined German armies invaded France. The war was the first in which both sides used railroads, the electrical telegraph, and rifled and breech-loading cannon and rifles — technological innovations that revolutionized warfare in the latter nineteenth century.

The Germans put in the field more than twice as many trained men as could the French: their logistics were superior, and they were distinctly better led. The French armies were defeated on the frontier and fell back, one army to the fortress city of Metz where it was surrounded and beseiged, another to Chalons, and another to Sedan, where it was trapped in an untenable position by the Germans. Napoleon, seeing that further resistance would be fruitless, took personal command and on September 2, 1870, surrendered the army of Sedan and himself to Bismarck. When the news reached Paris on September 4, imperial officials allowed the initiative to pass to republicans, who seized power and proclaimed the Third Republic. A new government, calling itself the Government of National Defense, carried on the war for another six months, during which Paris was besieged. Although the continuation of the war created a useful legend of

A sardonic commentary on the reign of Napoleon III by Honoré Daumier. Courtesy, Museum of Fine Arts, Boston.

republican vigor and patriotism, the outcome was never in doubt. An armistice ended the fighting on January 28, 1871, and a formal peace soon registered France's crushing defeat.

While the siege of Paris was going on, Bismarck won over the German states to joining a united Germany, and on January 18, 1871, the new German Empire was proclaimed in the Hall of Mirrors of the Palace of Versailles.

● Intellectual Ferment: Darwin and Marx

The nineteenth century European world produced a number of

intellectual giants — Charles Darwin, Karl Marx, John Stuart Mill, Soren Kierkegaard, Auguste Comte, Michael Faraday, Gregory Mendel, Louis Pasteur, Sigmund Freud, and some others — but the influence of none equalled that of the first two, Darwin and Marx.

Darwin was not a scientific genius like Isaac Newton, and his strictly scientific contribution was small. His *Origin of Species,* published in 1859, was no second *Principia* but a collection of evidence marshalled to support a borrowed theory. The theory was that new species of plants and animals are constantly evolving by a process of natural selection of those fit to survive in their particular environments. Philosophers, biologists, and geologists had advanced the evolutionary view of nature before Darwin. What was new in the *Origin of Species* was the careful elaboration of the theory and the presentation of supporting evidence so massive and so cogent that a rational challenge of the theory was virtually impossible. The book raised a popular furor because its thesis was clearly in conflict with the biblical story of the creation, which maintained that God had in the beginning created all species of plants and animals in final, unevolving form.

In 1859 Darwin applied his theory only to plants and animals, but in *The Descent of Man,* published in 1871, he included man in his evolutionary system. Extension of the system did not stop there. The social Darwinists applied the law of natural selection to society and to the economy. All life is a struggle, they said, and progress is achieved by the survival of the fittest and the elimination of the unfit by the process of natural selection. In effect, they confirmed the eighteenth-century Enlightenment's belief in natural law but repudiated the Enlightenment's principles of equality and fraternity. For a harmonious and beneficent nature they substituted a nature that was wasteful, savage, and ugly. Their ideas could be and were used to justify unscrupulous competition, the exploitation of the weak by the strong, the imperial rule of "lesser breeds," and a callous detachment on the part of governments.

Just as there were evolutionists before Darwin, so there were socialists before Marx. He took the ideas of the utopian socialists, added some significant elements, combined them with ideas of the classical economists, informed them with the insights of German idealist philosophy, and created "scientific socialism." His formulation of socialism largely shaped the doctrine and programs of socialist parties and by indirection also shaped policies of capitalist governments forced to face the challenge of socialism.

Marx maintained that the determining force in history is economic and that the essence of the historical process is the class struggle for possession and control of the means of production. In the nineteenth-century industrial and capitalist economy, Marx held, the worker produced more than he required for his subsistence, and the capitalist expropriated the surplus; this situation gave the class struggle its current form, a struggle between workers and capitalists. The expropriation of surplus value, moreover, concentrates wealth increasingly in the hands of a small oligarchy, and more and more of the population are forced down into the miserable proletariat. Eventually and inevitably the proletariat will rise in revolt, seize the means of production, and establish a classless and equitable society. Marx's analysis had great intellectual appeal because it appeared to be scientific in an age when science enjoyed great prestige. It had great attraction for all who hoped for drastic change in the economy and society, for it made socialism self-realizing and inevitable.

• Science and Technology

Although the nineteenth century produced no Copernicus or Newton, it was a century of expanding scientific activity and of discoveries that by the beginning of the twentieth century were undermining the comfortable, rational, orderly, predictable world of nature that had been part of every educated European's accepted beliefs since the seventeenth century. Wilhelm Wundt launched the science of experimental psychology; Ivan Pavlov, through his studies of conditioned reflexes, and Sigmund Freud in psychoanalysis, revealed that man's behavior is not necessarily determined by rational choice. The work of physicists in France such as Pierre and Marie Curie, J. J. Thomson and Lord Ernest Rutherford in England, and Max Planck and Albert Einstein in Germany, forced a revision of the Newtonian conception of matter as permanent and unchanging and imposed the recognition that the "laws of nature," cherished for two centuries, were not laws at all. Louis Pasteur and Robert Koch advanced and demonstrated the germ theory of disease, with practical consequences soon to be dramatically apparent in falling mortality rates.

Except for an occasional highly publicized discovery, the work of pioneering scientists was unknown except to a few initiates. The successful application of scientific discoveries in technology, however, touched the lives of millions. A glance at the history of technology in the latter nineteenth century and up to 1914 brings a striking realization of how many devices that shape our lives today are the creations of nineteenth-century scientists, engineers, and technicians: the Bessemer Converter and

Opening of the Paris to Orleans Railway, 1843. Courtesy, Cabinet des Estampes, Bibliotheque nationale, Paris.

the open hearth furnace, which made possible the production of steel at low cost and ushered in the Age of Steel, the transatlantic cable and the telephone, the typewriter, the rotary printing press, and the linotype, the steam turbine, the internal combustion engine, the gasoline automobile, and the airplane, the electric light, motion pictures, and the radio. This list alone suggests how great the world has changed since the nineteenth century began.

• Literature and Art

Romanticism continued to have its adherents even beyond mid-century, but realism, committed to the depiction of daily life as it really was, became the more influential school in literature. Among the greatest novelists of the century were Victor Hugo, Charles Dickens, George Eliot, Gustave Flaubert, Fedor Dostoevsky, and Leo Tolstoy, all of them except Hugo realists. Charles Baudelaire repudiated the forms and subject matter of romantic poetry and dared to write on forbidden subjects such as vice, decay, and corruption, and though he scandalized his contemporaries he turned poetry in new directions, so that he has been described as "the first modern poet." The rapid development of public education expanded the potential for an appreciation of this literature, and technological advances in printing made it more readily available. But despite optimistic predictions from the partisans of human progress, this literature, contemporary philosophy and music as well remained the preserve of a small elite. The newly literate masses read the penny press and "dime novels."

In painting Gustave Courbet had opened a new age of realism with his "The Burial at Ornans," exhibited in 1850. Beginning in the 1870s the French impressionists practiced their own form of realism — the meticulous depiction of light and color as it appeared in nature. Romantic music continued to flourish in the latter half of the century, especially in works of Richard Wagner. He combined poetry, national legends, and theater in his music-dramas and gave powerful expression to growing German nationalism.

18

Toward a New Upheaval

IN THE FORTY-FOUR YEARS after 1870 Europe was, we can now see, on the road to war. Although few Europeans realized the changed nature of warfare, already in the latter decades of the receding century some military men at least knew that when war came it would be deadly and destructive beyond all precedent. In the nineteenth century the industrial revolution had spread across Europe, and by 1914 the great powers, except Russia, were highly industrialized. Napoleon's armies moving slowly on foot and fighting with smooth-bore muskets were closer to the armies of the Renaissance than to those of the early twentieth century. Lord Nelson's cumbersome, wooden sailing fleet, armed with unrifled cannon, bore little resemblance to the steel armor-plated, steam-driven dreadnaughts of 1914 which carried great rifled artillery pieces. Nelson and Napoleon had been closer to the technology and the command problems of the Renaissance than to those of the early twentieth century.

● Economic and Social Conditions

Scientific and technological advances enabled Europe's industry to produce goods on a scale undreamed of at the century's beginning. Entirely new electrical and chemical industries rivaled in importance the older metallurgical industries. The steel industry profited from a series of newly invented techniques, especially the Bessemer Converter (1856) and the Siemens-Martin open hearth process (1867), which yielded high-grade steel at low cost. Steel production in Britain, France, and Germany quickly soared from 260,000 tons in 1865 to 23,000,000 tons in 1910. From this huge output came cheaper and safer rails, larger and more powerful ships, and stronger building materials. The use of steam power became more efficient with the introduction of multiple expansion engines after 1854 and of the steam turbine in the 1880s. In the chemical industry research led to many new products and to improvements in pharmaceuticals and in explosives. Iron and later steel ships, powered by fuel-efficient engines or turbines and equipped with refrigeration, brought a flood of low-cost food to Europe, forcing either a drastic readjustment of agriculture as in Britain which became dependent on imported food, or the raising of high tariff walls as in France.

Industrialization changed the appearance of much of the European landscape and altered the structure of society. Industrial towns and cities became part of the ordinary scene across the continent. The increasing demand for skilled workers contributed to the expansion of public education and the increase in literacy and in technical proficiency. Labor unions, which had been handicapped by various legal restrictions until the final decades of the century, had before the war become an important element in European politics. In Britain, unions had 3,500,000 members in 1912 and controlled the new and growing Labour party. French unions spurned political action, but in the decade before the war demonstrated their power by many successful strikes. In Germany the socialist and Christian unions with more than 2,500,000 members used both economic and political means to defend labor interests; the Social Democratic party, which drew its support chiefly from the socialist unions, grew to be the nation's largest party in 1912.

By 1914 industrial workers, especially in the more advanced Western countries, were beginning to share somewhat more in the fruits of industrialization; they ate better, dressed better, and had to do less brutally hard work than their fathers and grandfathers. Most, however, still lived in squalid slums that clustered around factories. Even the greatest urban renewal project of the century, the rebuilding of Paris in the 1850s and 1860s, had done little to improve workers' housing. Everywhere the dismal urban slums were rich breeding grounds of radical voters and socialist militants. The new European world was largely an urban society. By 1914 six European cities had populations in excess of one million. Two-thirds of England's population in 1914 lived in cities of 20,000 or more. Even in less urbanized countries, cities set the standards and fixed the tastes that people everywhere observed.

• Christianity in a Secular World

The long pontificate of Pius IX (1846-78) illustrates the dilemma of the Roman Catholic church and Christianity as a whole in an age when science, democracy, and socialism threatened their traditional foundations. Pius began his reign as a liberal reformer with the promise of trying to adapt the church to a changing world, but the experience of the Revolution of 1848, when he was coerced by radical revolutionaries and forced to flee from Rome, changed him into a reactionary determined to preserve and if necessary restore the traditional position and doctrines of the church. The loss of temporal power when part of the Papal States joined the Kingdom of Italy in 1861 moved Pius to seek compensation in increased spiritual influence. In 1864 he issued a *Syllabus of Errors,* a list in eighty articles of "the errors of our time," including nationalism, socialism, communism, free masonry, rationalism, and faith in science. An accompanying encyclical, *Quanta Cura,* condemned them all. Pius rejected religious toleration and freedom of conscience and insisted that the church control all schools. "It is an error to believe," he declared, "that the Roman Pontiff . . . ought to reconcile himself to progress, liberalism, and modern civilization." In 1869 he convened the first general council since the sixteenth century when the church faced the crisis of the Protestant revolt, and induced it to endorse *Quanta Cura* and to proclaim the dogma of papal infallibility: the dogma that when the pope speaks *ex cathedra,* his decisions on matters of faith and morals are infallible. These actions were a blow to Catholic liberals, who hoped to adapt the church to a changing world. The French and German bishops abstained from voting on papal infallibility. The Austrian government annulled its concordat with the papacy, and in Germany Bismarck, seeing in the new papal pretensions a potential threat to German unity, began an harrassment of the Catholic church in the empire.

The Roman church was not alone in having problems of adjustment to changing times. The implications of the Darwinian denial of the biblical story of the creation were as threatening to Protestant churches as to Catholic. No revealed religion, moreover, could be indifferent to the findings of cultural anthropoligists that the most sacred of Christian rites and ideas could be traced back to primitive societies and that historically religion was almost inextricably mixed with magic. Equally difficult were the findings and conclusions of biblical scholars that showed the Bible to be less than divine but filled with myths and inconsistencies. Moreover, the latter nineteenth century was an age of materialism. Increasingly people were becoming absorbed in material pursuits, and religion was becoming for most a minor part of their lives. Nationalism was developing into a veritable rival religion with its own pressing requirements of faith, service, and sacrifice.

Pius IX's successor, Leo XIII, continued to condemn liberalism and nationalism and to make broad claims for the church's obligation to direct all aspects of secular life, but he did disassociate the church from reactionary politics and encouraged Catholics to study science, maintaining that there was no conflict between true science and religion. Leo's greatest contribution to the renewal of the church was his bringing it into the struggle between labor and capital on the side of labor. His encyclical, *Rerum Novarum*, issued in 1891, defended private property but blamed capitalist employers for working-class poverty and exploitation. Employers as Christians had the moral duty, he said, to improve the condition of their workers. He expressed approval of socialism, though not of Marxism, and called on Catholics to form their own labor unions. This "workingman's pope" breathed new life into social Catholicism and narrowed the gap created by his predecessors between the church and the industrial, urban world of his time.

• Italy after Unification

The unifications of Italy and Germany after centuries of division were two of the great political developments of the nineteenth century, but actual unity proved to be elusive. Regional, economic, religious, linguistic, and class differences remained as serious obstacles to unity of national goals and policies.

In Italy the high hopes for a viable parliamentary democracy were disappointed. The south remained agrarian, its peasants living in poverty; real political power was exercised by virtually feudal landlords and the Mafia. It was a region scarcely assimilable into a parliamentary and democratic state. In the north industrialization brought new wealth, but it was ill-distributed, and workers protested in frequent violent strikes in the two decades before 1914.

The parliamentary system itself failed to function effectively. No strong political parties developed, and government was necessarily by precarious coalition, sustained by open corruption, a situation that made the resolution of the country's myriad problems almost impossible. The most effective prime ministers, Francesco Crispi and Giovanni Giolitti, who were in and out of power between 1887 and 1914, did accomplish some useful social and educational reforms, but both sought to distract public attention from domestic ills by colonial conquest in Africa and in doing so diverted the country's resources into wasteful wars. Growing popular disaffection was demonstrated after the establishment of universal manhood suffrage in 1912 by the growing strength of radical parties on both the right and the left.

● Germany after Unification

Bismarck wrote into the constitution of the new German Empire some elements of parliamentary democracy, but the new state was nonetheless conservative and authoritarian. Real political power was in the hands of the King of Prussia and German Emperor, the landed aristocracy (who together imposed the stamp of Prussian militarism on united Germany) and the wealthy bourgeoisie. But even this combination was scarcely equal to coping with the problems of rapidly growing and still divided Germany. National minorities — more than two million Poles, thousands of Danes, Alsatians, and others — were still within German borders. The particularism of the Catholic south German states was still very much alive. Catholics, a third of the population, were suspicious of Protestant Prussia. Aristocratic landowners of Prussia feared the loss of their influence by being forced to share authority with new, emerging power groups. The rapid industrialization after 1870 produced a large and disaffected proletariat.

By the turn of the century Germany had become the world's second most productive industrial power, and by 1914 she was passing Britain in some areas of industry. She then produced more steel than all the rest of Europe combined, and her chemical and electrical industries led the world. Her merchants, supported by the German banks, moved aggressively into markets around the world. Hamburg and Bremen became teeming international ports and the bases of great ocean shipping companies. The country's burgeoning wealth could support a larger population, and between 1871 and 1914 it rose from thirty-eight million to sixty-eight million making Germany the most populous state in Europe after Russia. These developments had immense political consequences. At home they challenged the supremacy of the landed aristocracy, which had dominated Germany for centuries. Abroad they challenged the industrial and commercial supremacy of Britain.

In the 1870s Bismarck discerned two principal and grave threats to Germany's new-found national unity. German Catholics and German socialists, in his judgment, had extra-national loyalties that made them at least potentially disloyal to Germany, and he undertook to break their political power. In the so-called *Kulturkampf* he dissolved most Catholic orders, expelled the Jesuits from the empire, made civil marriage obligatory, brought the training and the discipline of Catholic clergy in Prussia under state control, and suspended state financial support of all defiant priests. The Anti-Socialist Law, first passed in 1878 and in force until 1890, banned meetings, publications, and money-raising by the

Kaiser William in Field Uniform.

Social Democratic party but did not bar it from elections or its deputies from the Reichstag. Parallel with this repressive policy Bismarck sought to win the working class away from the socialists by demonstrating that the state could do more for workers than the socialists could. Between 1883 and 1887 he secured approval of legislation that gave Germany the most advanced system of social security in the world. It included insurance against sickness, accident, old age, and disability, financed jointly by the state, employers, and workers.

Bismarck was himself a product of the old agrarian and rural Germany of noble landlords and peasants, and he wanted to preserve as much of it as possible. The young Emperor William II, who came to the throne in 1888, was a man of a new age, although he did retain some of the illusions of divine right rule. Willful and impulsive, he dismissed Bismarck from the chancellorship in 1890, abrogated the Anti-Socialist Law (Bismarck had already ended the *Kulturkampf*), and abandoned Bismarck's carefully balanced defensive foreign policy. He gave his support to all those forces that were ambitious to make Germany a great world and colonial power. As part of this effort and also for reasons of internal political advantage, Germany began in 1898 to build a large, high seas battle fleet, an enterprise that Britain saw not only as a menace to her commerce but as a threat to her very existence, dependent as it was on sea-borne food supplies. The principal opposition to the new belligerence came from the Social Democratic party. It had survived the repression of

The Avenue de l'Opéra in Paris lit up by electricity in 1878. From *La Lumière Electrique*, 1881.

the 1870s and 1880s, and in the elections of 1912 won more seats in the Reichstag than any other party. As it grew in power and wealth, however, the party ceased to be revolutionary or even very radical. Had it been inclined to restrain the government, the absence of ministerial responsibility to parliament would have prevented effective action. Even in 1914 the ministry was answerable only to the emperor.

• France after 1870

Before the National Assembly elected in 1871 could turn — gratuitously, because it was elected only to make peace — to deciding on the future government of France, it had to cope with civil war. Parisians, outraged by seemingly anti-Parisian acts of the provisional government at Versailles, revolted, organized an independent municipal government, the Commune of Paris, and called on citizens of other French cities to follow their example. Adolphe Thiers, head of the provisional government, reassembled scattered French troops, and in May attacked and conquered Paris in savage fighting on both sides that left some 30,000 dead. Although the commune was only marginally socialist in either membership or actions, Karl Marx in his contemporary pamphlet, *The Civil War in France,* called it "a working class government ... the political form at last discovered under which to work out the emancipation of labor." For more than a century it has occupied an important place in socialist and communist legend and doctrine.

Monarchists held a majority of the seats in the National Assembly, and they intended to restore the monarchy in France. They were frustrated by being split between Legitimists, who would restore the Bourbon Count of Chambord, and Orleanists, who would place Louis-Philippe's grandson on the throne. The uncompromising stance of Chambord prevented an agreement between the two groups. While the monarchists temporized, hoping that time would bring a solution to their problems, republicans gathered strength, and by 1875 a majority in the assembly was willing to approve a republican constitution. The Constitutional Laws adopted in 1875 legally established the Third French Republic and provided for its continuation. In elections over the next five years, republicans won control of the Chamber of Deputies, the Senate, and the Presidency. The elections registered the shift of political power away from the notables who had dominated France since 1815, the landed aristocracy and gentry and the financial magnates, to the middle bourgeoisie of substantial businessmen and professional men. The latter combination dominated French political life for two decades, until around 1900, when the petty bourgeoisie, represented by the Radical party, won a hold on the reins of power.

Until about 1905 the Third Republic was occupied largely with defending itself against forces that would destroy it, the monarchists, Bonapartists, militant Catholics, and ultra-nationalists. In the early 1880s it struck at the Catholic church's power over youth by making primary education compulsory and free and banning religious education in the public schools. Later in the 1880s it frustrated the efforts of the popular General Georges Boulanger and his reactionary supporters to win control of the government and to change the constitution. In the 1890s the Dreyfus Affair brought new and more ominous threats to the Republic. Captain Alfred Dreyfus, a Jewish officer attached to the General Staff, was convicted of treason on dubious evidence and by illegal procedures and shipped off to the penal colony in French Guiana. The efforts of his family and friends, who discovered the irregularities of his trial, to reopen the case divided the country into two bitterly opposed camps. The anti-Dreyfusards insisted that any questioning of the army's omniscience and judgment was a threat to national security and to society itself. The Dreyfusards held that justice must be done to the individual regardless of the consequences for any institution. The former group recruited its following from enemies of the Republic, including many of the Catholic clergy; the latter recruited its supporters from the Republic's defenders.

For a time the Republic appeared to be in danger, but in 1899 a coalition government, the Government of Republican Defense, reopened the case, and the courts eventually pronounced Dreyfus innocent. The government went on to republicanize the officer's corps of the army, to separate church and state, to dissolve most religious orders, and to ban teaching by any religious order.

With these accomplishments, completed in 1905, the Third Republic had disposed of the principal enemies that had threatened it since 1875. During its first three decades, when it was preoccupied with assuring its own survival, it had neglected the growing problems of an increasingly industrialized and urbanized society, and it had fallen behind Germany and Britain in dealing with these problems. After 1905 it had to face up to them. This was especially difficult because the working class had been alienated by decades of hostility and neglect. French organized labor rejected parliamentary methods and put its faith in confrontation and violence. The decade preceding 1914 brought an epidemic of strikes and little progress toward greater social justice.

• Britain after 1868

The politics of the quarter century after 1868 in Britain were dominated by two men, William Gladstone and Benjamin Disraeli, who between them held the office of prime minister for nineteen years. Gladstone was a liberal and a zealous, righteous reformer; Disraeli a conservative more interested in diplomacy and empire than in domestic affairs. Both were anxious to narrow the breach between the ruling elite of aristocracy and upper bourgeoisie and the rest of the population. To this end Gladstone established a national system of primary schools, opened the civil service to all through competitive examinations, ended the purchase of army commissions, and extended the suffrage to include almost all adult males. Disraeli put through legislation requiring improved conditions in factories and mines, provided for low-cost public housing, and made sanitary codes more effective, but it was also he who purchased control of the Suez Canal for Britain, made Queen Victoria Empress of India, and by adroit use of British naval power in the Mediterranean won a key role for himself and Britain in the Congress of Berlin in 1878 and in settlement of the Russian-Turkish-Austrian conflict in the Balkans.

These years were the apogee of British power. Britain was the most powerful industrial nation in the world. The volume of her foreign trade and the size of her merchant marine were unmatched. Her investments encircled the globe. Her empire was the largest ever known, and the Royal Navy ruled the seas. And the wealth of the world poured into this one small island. The one obvious cloud in these fair skies was the Irish Question. The English had oppressed and exploited Ireland since the mid-seventeenth century, and embittered Irish nationalists now demanded independence. Parliament, however, would not even agree to Gladstone's twice proposed Home Rule, under which the Irish would be allowed to manage their own domestic affairs while subject to the British crown and its foreign policy. The problem was still unresolved when England went to war in 1914.

The last two decades before the war were marked by growing concern with the problems of the working class, a concern induced by the agitation of left-wing intellectuals, the growing influence of trade unions, and especially, after 1900, by the political clout of the Labour party. The liberal government that came to power in 1906 launched an ambitious program of social legislation, and before 1914 it had won passage of a Workingmen's Compensation Law and a Minimum Wage Law and established a comprehensive system of old age pensions, sickness insurance, and unemployment insurance. These programs combined with heavy expenditures on the naval construction forced the government to find extraordinary sources of revenue, and David Lloyd George, the Chancellor of the Exchequer, submitted to Parliament in 1908 a budget that would impose heavy new taxes on incomes, inheritance, and unearned increments of land values. The rich and privileged were outraged, and the House of Lords rejected the budget, defying the Commons' traditional control of taxation. This defiance led to the passage of the Parliament Bill of 1911 that formally deprived the Lords of power to veto money bills and restricted their power over other legislation to delaying action. This diminution of the great strong-hold of the aristocracy stands as a symbolic capping of the process of democratization of British government and society begun with the Reform Bill of 1832.

• Russia after 1881

The violent end of Alexander II at the hands of anarchists contributed to making his son and successor, Alexander III, a zealous reactionary. He sought to repudiate his father's liberalism and to return to the autocracy, Orthodoxy, and nationalism of his grandfather, Nicholas I. Radical organizations were broken up or driven underground. Local judicial and administrative powers were restored to the nobility. National minorities were forcibly assimilated and religious dissenters prosecuted, while anti-Semitism became an official policy. Coming at a time when economic and social changes were beginning to demolish the ancient structure of Russian society, Alexander's policy was a hopeless anachronism.

The emancipation of the serfs in 1861 had opened the road to industrialization by providing a free and more mobile labor force, but before much progress could be made, railroads had to be built and credit institutions and a stable currency established. By the late 1880s these preparations were well advanced, and the first phase of Russia's industrial revolution began. Between 1885 and 1900 the index of industrial production tripled. With this came a rapid increase of population and a shift from country to city. But at the turn of the century more people were still trying to live on the land than the land in the current state of technology could support. Lack of capital, land management that was essentially medieval, antiquated tools and methods, and simple ignorance made change difficult. Yields were low and poverty widespread.

Nicholas II, who succeeded Alexander III in 1894, was well-intentioned but benighted in his political convictions and not very astute, certainly not the leader required to deal with the rising tide of discontent that touched every class. A disasterous war against Japan in 1904 brought accumulating troubles to a head. The Revolution of 1905 forced the tsar to grant a constitution guaranteeing civil liberties and providing for a national parliament, the Duma. Once the revolutionary crisis had passed, the government returned to many of its reactionary ways, but the country did now have a representative assembly where grievances could be expressed and occasionally remedial action forced. The government canceled the remaining peasant redemption dues. In 1907-08 the ministry of Count Pierre Stolypin, hoping to create a class of independent peasant proprietors, issued edicts that ended the ties that bound individual peasants to the communes and permitted them to take their share of communal land in enclosed privately-held farms. Stolypin called the effort "a wager on the strong." It was a bold attempt to change the habits of centuries and to create a conservative peasantry as a bulwark against revolution. In 1917 the great peasant revolution would show that the "wager on the strong" had failed.

The seizure of power in 1917 by the Bolshevik faction of the Russian Social Democratic party suggests that the Marxian socialists had an importance in pre-war Russia that in fact they did not enjoy. Before 1917 the Social Democrats were not taken very seriously, for they were a party dedicated to proletarian revolution in a country where there was scarcely any proletariat. Apparently much more threatening to the status quo was the Social Revolutionary party. It was preparing for a peasant revolution in a country still overwhelmingly composed of peasants, most of them land-hungry and disgruntled.

● The New Imperialism

The first great age of European expansion closed with the ending of the last colonial war between Britain and France in 1763 and the revolt of the British North American colonies in 1776. For the next one hundred years the European powers, preoccupied with revolution and wars at home and with industrial development and reforms, were little interested in acquiring colonies. About 1880, however, a new age of European imperialism began. In the succeeding two decades European countries added ten million square miles and 150 million people to their colonial holdings. Britain led the way, acquiring control of the Suez Canal in 1875 and in 1876 making its first effort to establish its rule over South Africa. In the succeeding years the British extended their rule to embrace Egypt, the Sudan, Kenya, most of South Africa, and various holdings on the African west coast. The French, who had lost most of their empire to the British a century earlier, were disturbed by the British move into Egypt, a traditional French sphere, and in the early 1880s they began to stake their claims in West Africa, a move that eventually culminated in the formation of two huge colonies, French Equatorial Africa and French West Africa. They also moved into Madagascar, Morocco, and Tunisia and tightened their hold, first established by Napoleon III, on Indochina. Bismarck at first spurned colonial expansion for Germany and encouraged France to divert her belligerence and waste her resources in this foolish activity, but in 1885 he sanctioned the establishment of a German protectorate over territory in East Africa and over the Cameroons in the west. Italy moved into the Horn of Africa and Tripoli. Russia in the 1890s shifted the focus of her imperial expansion from the Ottoman Empire to east Asia and began penetration into Manchuria and Korea. A weak China attracted the imperial interest of colony-hungry powers, and Britain, France, Germany, and Russia established "spheres of influence" with special trading privileges within her boundaries.

The Europeans' superior technology, especially in weapons, made the conquest of colonies relatively easy. European rule once established was exploitive and often cruel, despite pretensions of bringing civilization and Christianity to backward peoples. No respect was shown for native cultures, and no effort made to preserve native crafts and arts. Some few individuals and companies made huge fortunes in the colonies, and others found in them satisfaction of ambitions for power, but generally colonies, because they required heavy expenditure on administration, police, and defense, were a drain on the mother country.

- **Imperialism's Motives**

The motives of the great outburst of colonial expansion in the nineteenth century were so mixed as to defy separation and weighing. For long the conventional explanation was that European industrial nations had expanded their productivity beyond the capacity of home markets to consume its products and were consequently obliged to seek markets overseas. Similarly surplus capital in Europe sought more profitable investment in colonies, and colonies, too, could furnish valuable raw materials, such as rubber from the Congo and diamonds from South Africa. National pride and ambition also played a part. Colonies were a mark of prestige, and when one power added to its holdings, others felt obliged to add to theirs. Jules Ferry, prime minister in France in the early 1880s, declared that for France to abandon colonial expansion would be to abdicate her position as a great power. William II's chancellor, Bernhard von Bülow, insisted that Germany should have its place in the sun.

In some cases colonial victories were compensation for reverses or failure at home. Once an empire was begun, its defense and an assured access to the various colonies required acquisition of other territories for naval bases, shipyards, and coaling stations. Social Darwinism provided an intellectual justification, depicting white Europeans as the most fit of races and its subjugation and even elimination of "lesser breeds" part of an inevitable and beneficial natural process. For thousands of more humane men and women the call to serve and to improve the health and the living standards of native peoples was felt as a very real moral obligation. Christian missionaries were not simply precursors of soldiers and traders. Finally, no explanation of imperialism can be complete without recognition that much of it was simply the work of individual men, often quite independent of home governments but ambitious for power and for adventure that they could not find in Europe.

- **Background of the First World War:**
  The Emerging European Alliances

For two decades after 1870 the international scene in Europe was dominated by Bismarck. He had accomplished his goals for Prussia and Germany and believed that renewed war could only be detrimental to German interests. He was determined to keep the peace, and since he saw France as the most likely disturber of the peace, he undertook to make war impractical for her by confronting her with a very large German army and by depriving her of possible allies. Britain, committed to "splendid isolation," could be counted out, but Bismarck sought to join all the other European powers with Germany. In 1873 he formed the Three Emperors' League, composed of Russia, Austria-Hungry, and Germany, and associated Italy with it. In 1881 it became the more binding Three Emperors' Alliance, which remained in force until 1887. This alliance had the additional purpose of preventing a clash between Russia and Austria in the Balkans. In 1879 Bismarck had concluded a bilateral alliance with Austria-Hungary, the Dual Alliance, which remained the cornerstone of Germany's diplomatic system until the collapse of both empires in 1918. When Russia refused to renew the Three Emperors' Alliance in 1887, Bismarck kept her tied to Germany by the secret Reinsurance Treaty. Three years later, however, the new emperor, William II, dismissed Bismarck and allowed the Reinsurance Treaty to lapse.

The government of the Third French Republic had early understood that its most effective guarantee against renewed German aggression would be an alliance with Russia. The threat of a war on two fronts, which this alliance would raise for Germany, would be a powerful deterrent, and if war should come, there would be an eastern front to draw much of the German army away from France's frontier. Early in the 1880s the French had made overtures to Russia but received no encouragement from St. Petersburg, where the ultra-conservative leadership was not disposed to join forces with the most dangerously revolutionary and atheistic country in Europe. But in the latter 1880s and in 1890 the Russians became disposed to listen to the French proposals by the French government's sanctioning of massive sales of Russian bonds on the French market, when other money markets were closed to them, and by the new coolness of William's Germany. The result, in 1891, was an entente, an agreement to consult on common defense against German attack, which in 1894 became a formal alliance. The German General Staff reacted by changing its war plans. Assuming that Russia's mobilization would be slow, the German staff planned, in event of war, a quick, massive blow at France to knock her out of the war. This accomplished, the German armies would turn about and deal with Russian armies in the east. For France this meant that if her eastern ally went to war with Germany, even over a dispute in the east far from French frontiers, France would receive the first and full brunt of the German army's might.

In 1898 Germany embarked on the construction of a big navy. The decision to do so was made as much for internal political advantage as for military reasons, but it contributed significantly to dividing Europe into two hostile, armed camps. Britain saw the growing German fleet as a mortal threat, and the government changed its diplomatic and defense policies to meet the threat. In 1904 Britain settled her outstanding imperial differences with France, and in 1907 made a similar settlement with Russia. Britain, France, and Russia were then united in the Triple Entente, facing the Triple Alliance of Germany, Austria-Hungary, and Italy. German testing of the Anglo-French entente in the Moroccan crises of 1905 and 1911 brought the two western powers closer together and moved them to begin joint military and naval planning for defense against Germany, giving the entente the attributes of an alliance.

• General Causes of the War

No single, simple explanation can show why the great European powers after 1870 formed permanent military alliances in time of peace for the first time in modern history, poured their resources into armaments, and eventually joined in suicidal war. Commercial rivalries exacerbated relations between countries, but they knew that they were each others' best customers. Colonial conflicts created national hostilities, but the colonial confrontations that threatened war were all settled, and when war came in 1914, it was over a European dispute. The collision of Russian and Austro-Hungarian expansion in the Balkans was lethal, but it did not necessarily imply a general European war. France and Germany were suspicious of each other's aggressive intentions, but in France by 1900 only a handful of zealots still wanted a war of revenge on Germany. Nationalism in the Balkans provided the igniting spark in 1914, but other forces fanned it into flame. Military leaders, prisoners of their own intricate plans, pushed civilian statesmen to mobilize armies lest the enemy win an advantage in time, and this handicapped the search for peaceful settlement. The German General Staff, moreover, wanted war in 1914, believing that Germany could win a war then but would soon lose its advantage if war were postponed. Finally the jingo press excited public nationalist feeling against neighbors and encouraged political leaders to regard war as politically advantageous.

• Immediate Causes of the War

The provoking incident in 1914 was the assassination on June 28 of the heir to the Austro-Hungarian throne, the Archduke Franz Ferdinand, and his wife by Bosnian nationalists, who feared that his plans for reform of the empire would frustrate hopes for a Greater Serbia. The Austrian government was divided on how to respond to the provocation, but the German government, pushed by the German General Staff, promised support for strong measures against Serbia, whose government was charged with collusion in the assassination. On July 28 Austria declared war on

Serbia. Russia, the protector of Slavs in the Balkans, prepared to aid Serbia. In a Balkan crisis in 1908-09 Russia had, under German pressure, backed down from her support of Serbia against Austria; her leaders in July 1914 reasoned that Russia could not back down again and retain any prestige or influence in the Balkans. France, anxious that no disagreement with Russia weaken the Franco-Russian alliance, made no effort to restrain her ally. The British government proposed several plans for settlement of the emerging dispute between Austria and Russia, but all were rejected or deflected by Berlin. On July 30 the tsar, under heavy pressure from his high command, ordered mobilization of the Russian army, and then the complex, rigid military plans took over in every country. Germany and France began mobilization of their armies on August 1. Germany declared war on Russia that same day and on France on August 3. The next day, when Germany failed to reply to Britain's demand that she withdraw her forces from Belgium, Britain joined France and Russia in the war. Of the great powers only Italy remained neutral.

Europe after one hundred years without a general conflict had gone to war. The Great Century with all its hopes for a golden age was about to end on the bloody fields of Flanders and Verdun, the swamps of Passchendaele, and the bleak plains of Poland and Russia. Said Sir Edward Grey, the British Foreign Secretary, on the day Britain declared war on Germany, "The lamps are going out all over Europe."

Suggestions for Further Reading

The students seeking a more comprehensive survey of the history of Europe in the nineteenth century should see R.R. Palmer and Joel Colton, *A History of the Modern World* (4th ed. 1971).

Century-long treatments of particular aspects of European history 1815-1914 are available. On industrialization two useful books are W.O. Henderson, *The Industrialization of Europe (1780-1914)* (1959) and David S. Landes, *The Unbound Prometheus. Technological Change and Industrial Development in Western Europe from 1750 to the Present* (1969). The spread of western European technology and capital across the continent is the subject of Rondo Cameron, *France and the Economic Development of Europe, 1800-1914* (1968). Social consequences of the industrial revolution are examined in Peter N. Stearns, *European Society in Upheaval. Social History since 1800* (1967) and in Jerome Blum, *The End of the Old Order in Rural Europe* (1978). The reactions of workers, intellectuals, and churches may be studied in E. P. Thompson, *The Making of the English Working Class* (1964), George Lichtheim, *A Short History of Socialism* (1970), Robert Heilbronner, *The Worldly Philosophers*

(1953), and J.L. Altholz, *The Churches in the Nineteenth Century* (1966). A number of fairly concise national histories span the century. David Thomson, *England in the Nineteenth Century* (1964), Gordon Wright, *France in Modern Times, from the Enlightenment to the Present* (2d ed., 1974), Hajo Holborn, *A History of Modern Germany* (1959-69), Vol. II, 1648-1840, Vol. III, 1840-1945, A.J.B.Whyte, *The Evolution of Modern Italy* (1965), Stanley C. Payne, *Politics and the Military in Modern Spain* (1967), C. A. McCartney, *The Habsburg Empire, 1790-1918* (1969), and B. H. Sumner, *A Short History of Russia* (1943). M. F. Anderson, *The Eastern Question, 1774-1923* (1966) surveys the evolution of a vexing diplomatic problem that divided Europe throughout the century.

The first decades after 1815, the subject of Chapter 16, can be profitably studied in F.B. Artz, *Revolution and Reaction, 1814-1832* (1934) and William L. Langer, *Political and Social Upheaval, 1832-1852* (1964), which take all Europe for their subjects, and in Theodore Hamerow, *Restoration, Revolution, and Reaction. Economics and Politics in Germany, 1815-1871* (1958), Marc Raeff, *The Decembrist Movement* (1966), and Nicholas Riasanovsky, *Nicholas I and Official Nationality in Russia, 1825-1855* (1959).

On the middle decades of the century, the subject of Chapter 17, the interested student will find many good, specialized books. The Revolutions of 1848 have inspired scores of volumes. Priscilla Robertson, *The Revolutions of 1848: A Social History* (1952) and William L. Langer, *Revolutions of 1848* (1969) are useful syntheses. On Victorian England a student could well begin with G.M. Young, *Victorian England: Portrait of an Age* (1964), Asa Briggs, *Victorian People. A Reassessment of Persons and Themes, 1851-1867* (1954), and, by the same author, *Victorian Cities* (1965). On the changing France of mid-century J.P.T. Bury, *Napoleon III and the Second French Empire* (1964) is a brief but reliable introduction, and Napoleon III's most lasting accomplishment is the subject of David H. Pinkney, *Napoleon III and the Rebuilding of Paris* (1958, 1972). Roger L. Williams, *The French Revolution of 1870-1871* (1969) puts the Paris Commune in historical perspective. On the emergence of united Germany the student should turn to Theodore Hamerow, *Restoration, Revolution, and Reaction* cited above, Otto Pflanze, *Bismarck and the Development of Germany: The Period of Unification, 1815-1871* (1963), and Lawrence Steefel, *Bismarck, the Hohenzollern Candidacy, and the Origins of the Franco-German War of 1870* (1962). Russia before and in the age of the Great Reforms can be studied in Jerome Blum, *Lord and Peasant in Russia from the Ninth to the Nineteenth Century* (1961) and W.E. Mosse, *Alexander II and the Modernization of Russia* (1959). C. Woodham-Smith, *The Reason Why* not only explains why the Light Cavalry Brigade made its suicidal charge in the Crimean War but also gives a perceptive picture of English society in mid-century. On intellectual developments of the middle decades the student should consult Gertrude Himmelfarb, *Darwin and the Darwinian Revolution* (1959) and Jacques Barzun, *Darwin, Marx, Wagner. A Critique of a Heritage* (1941).

The final decades of the nineteenth century and the years on to 1914, dealt with in Chapter 18, are the subject of two useful syntheses: Carlton J. H. Hayes, *A Generation of Materialism, 1871-1900* (1941) and Oran J. Hale, *The Great Illusion, 1900-1914* (1971). On the final flowering of the British Empire the curious student should read Donald Read, *Edwardian England, 1901-1915. Society and Politics* (1972) and George Dangerfield's intriguing *The Strange Death of Liberal England* (1946). The final decades of the Russian Empire are well treated in Hugh Seton-Watson, *The Decline of Imperial Russia, 1855-1914* (1952). Guy Chapman, *The Dreyfus Case* (1955) is a well-balanced account of that celebrated affair in France. Important contemporary developments in intellectual history are brilliantly discussed in H. Stuart Hughes, *Consciousness and Society: The Reorientation of European Social Thought, 1890-1930* (1958).

The search for the causes of the World War of 1914-1918 has produced an abundance of books. A newcomer to the subject would do well to begin with Sidney B. Fay, *The Origins of the World War* (2 vols, 1930), the first great classic on the subject, and go on to the more recent A.J.P. Taylor, *The Struggle for Mastery in Europe, 1848-1914* (1954), and Lawrence Lafore, *The Long Fuse. An Interpretation of the Origins of World War I* (1965). Fritz Fischer, *Germany's Aims in the First World War* (1967) is an influential and controversial work based on archives first revealed after the defeat of Germany in 1945. On imperialism the student should turn to Raymond F. Betts, *Europe Overseas. Phases of Imperialism* (1968) and on the related issue of nationalism to Boyd C. Shafer, *Nationalism. Myth and Reality* (1955). Edward R. Tannenbaum, *1900. The Generation before the Great War* (1977) presents a picture of life in Europe on the eve of the storm.

A student who would like to sample the new social and quantitative history might well read Charles Tilly, Louise Tilly, and Richard Tilly, *The Rebellious Century, 1830-1930* (1975); Joan W. Scott and Louise Tilly, "Women's Work and the Family in Nineteenth Century Europe," *Comparative Studies in Society and History,* XVII (1975), 36-64; and Theresa M. McBride, *The Domestic Revolution: The Modernization of Household Service in England and France, 1820-1920* (1976).

DEATH OF AN OLD WORLD
1914-1945

19

The Beginning of the End: World War I and an Unsuccessful Peace Settlement

SCARCELY ANYONE foresaw the holocaust of the First World War. Before it ended, the incredibly destructive war which lasted from 1914 to 1918 had devastated all of the belligerent nations and caused such ruin that European civilization never totally recovered. This war was a new phenomenon — a mass, industrial war draining all the energies of a nation and involving total populations, civilian and military alike. Ultimately it engaged most of the independent states of the world. Europe was no longer insular — the imperialistic ventures of the nineteenth century had drawn the entire globe into the European orbit.

• The Belligerents

At the outset the opposing camps — the Allied and the Central Powers — possessed reasonably equal military advantages. The Central Powers — Germany, Austria-Hungary, Bulgaria and Turkey — had a combined population of 150,000,000; the Allied and Associated Powers had 300,000,000. From first to last, the Central Powers mustered 21,000,000 soldiers, the Allied Powers 40,000,000. The Allied superiority in manpower, however, was offset by the weakness of Russia's industry — most of the Russian soldiers were poorly armed and easily mowed down by German machine guns. Nevertheless, the Allies had other advantages. Their ability to draw on their colonial possessions vastly increased their potential for a sustained war. England's control of the shipping lanes greatly facilitated Allied endeavors to draw men, food, and war material directly into the conflict. The Central Powers, on the other hand, suffered from shortages in all natural resources except coal and iron.

The Central Powers gained a significant advantage from their location at the center of Europe. They had considerably less difficulty with communication, not only because of interior lines but also because of the linguistic and cultural affinities between Germany and Austria-Hungary. The efficiency of the German military machine and coordination of the war effort strengthened their fighting potential. Throughout the first years of the war, England, France, and Russia cooperated with difficulty, which seriously hampered their military effectiveness. The problem of collaboration among the Allies was not satisfactorily resolved until 1918. By that time Russia had been removed from the coalition by revolution at home and the United States had taken her place, a decisive turning point in the war.

• The Failure of the Schlieffen Plan and the Stalemated War

The German government had recognized and feared for decades the possibility of a two-front war against France and England in the West and Russia in the East. To cope with this contingency a German Chief of Staff, General Alfred von Schlieffen, had drawn up a plan for a short war, based on a quick victory over France before England could come to her assistance and then, keeping only a small German force in the West, a concentrated attack and quick defeat of Russia. The Schlieffen Plan called for the main German striking force to hit France through Belgium and then to drive straight to the channel coast to prevent British forces from landing. The German army would then swing around Paris, separate the capital and the government from the rest of the country and catch the French army in a pincer grip. The plan nearly succeeded. England did not declare war until August 4 when German forces were already in Belgium, but the Belgian fortresses held out longer than the Germans expected. The Schlieffen Plan failed primarily because the Belgian's delaying tactics allowed the British to rush troops quickly to France's aid and because, at a crucial moment, a Russian invasion in the East caused the Germans to withdraw several divisions from the western front. The Russians as well as the British had mobilized their armies far more rapidly than the German strategists had believed possible.

Europe – 1914
- European Allied Countries
- The Central Powers
- Neutral Countries

The failure of the initial German offensive was the first indication that victory would not be easy for either side. The British and the French maintained a stubborn resistance to repeated German onslaughts. Neither side won a clear-cut victory at the First Battle of the Marne in September, 1914. The opposing armies held their positions, dug into long ditches protected by barbed wire and a stretch of continually-shelled territory called "no-man's land." Germany had failed to prevent the two-front war and settled down to trench warfare on both her eastern and western fronts.

Throughout 1915 and 1916 the war remained a stalemate while the trenches were extended from the channel coast to the Swiss border — 500 miles of ditches where men lived like animals. In the East the lines extended fully 1200 miles. More and more troops were hurled into futile assaults and the trenches became more elaborate as armies, kitchens, hospitals, and command areas moved underground. Men learned to exist with mud, human waste, ice, and the putrid smell of bloated, unburied bodies of the dead. Artillery fire constantly threatened – on a twenty-mile section of the front an army might fire 6,000,000 artillery shells in one month (in some places there was one gun for every nine yards of front) Life expectancy in the trenches dropped to less than six months for privates and to about two months for lieutenants as millions of soldiers died on the western front without succeeding in moving the lines more than seven miles in either direction. The populations of Europe decimated their youth, destroyed their leadership, and drained their economies in a war which neither side could win. At the Battle of Verdun in 1916, 700,000 men were killed or wounded and the Battle of the Somme in the same year caused one million casualties. On the eastern front, in one single offensive in Galicia, the Russians lost two million men. Where the fighting was heaviest in France, the topsoil was simply blown away – and the land became a desert. Lice, flies, and rats spread disease in both armies, killing nearly as many people as the bullets.

● The British Blockade

Although there was only one major naval battle, the war at sea proved to be decisive to the final outcome. The Battle of Jutland, the only serious engagement, was a tactical victory for the Germans but a strategic victory for the British; the German navy extensively damaged the British naval forces, but after the battle the German fleet never again left its home ports and the British continued to control vast stretches of ocean. British ships imposed a tight naval blockade around Germany, limiting the ability of the Central Powers to import war materials and food. So effectively did the British succeed in cutting off Germany's food supplies that malnutrition reached epic proportions – the German people were to remember for years the "Turnip Winter" of 1916.

In order to break the British blockade, the German navy developed a new weapon, the submarine, which seriously challenged British naval superiority. The Germans never had more than sixty submarines operating at any one time, however, and the Allies were able to develop anti-submarine defenses which diminished their effectiveness. German foolhardiness in employing without restraint a weapon which antagonzied not only the belligerent but also the neutral nations was a major factor causing the final defeat of the Central Powers. As early as 1915 the Germans began unrestricted submarine warfare, attacking not only British ships, but those of neutral nations. In May, 1915 the English passenger ship *Lusitania* was torpedoed and sunk, killing more than a thousand civilians, including

A Germany Company at Rest, from an etching by Otto Dix.
Courtesy, Museum of Fine Arts, Boston.

many women and children (more than a hundred were Americans). President Woodrow Wilson made it clear to Germany that such acts would force the United States into the war, and for nearly two years the Germans discontinued their attacks against noncombatant shipping. However, in January, 1917 Germany's military situation forced her to resume attacks against all shipping, and during that year German submarines sank nearly 3,000 ships, including American and other neutral vessels. Unrestricted

German submarine warfare brought the United States into the war on April 6, 1917. By that time Allied sub-chasers, depth charges, and the convoy system allowed American ships to carry two million American soldiers successfully into the European war.

The Russians, struggling with revolution at home, had removed themselves from the war in March, 1918 when the Bolsheviks signed the Treaty of Brest-Litovsk, ceding vast Russian territories to the Germans. The two-front war was over, and Germany was able to concentrate her full military attention on the western front. The Americans arrived barely in time to meet the all-out German offensive in 1918.

• America Enters the War

During the years of the stalemate which reduced the economic resources of both the Allied and Central Powers, the United States had experienced a period of unprecedented economic growth and expansion. America brought all her wealth and power to the war effort and brought as well American soldiers fired with a new zeal, a determination to defeat the German Kaiser and "make the world safe for democracy." Their enthusiasm injected fresh energy into the war-weary British and French fighting men. The Americans, too, contributed a powerful new weapon, President Woodrow Wilson's Fourteen Point Plan for peace, which in the winter of 1918 demanded a "peace without victory" and had a powerful appeal to the war-weary in Germany. The Fourteen Points called for freedom of the seas, the development of free trade, armaments reduction, national self-determination, the creation of a League of Nations to keep the peace, and an end to secret diplomacy and secret treaties. With her allies rapidly capitulating in the east and internal revolution brewing at home, the German High Command urged the government to sue for peace on the basis of the Fourteen Points. In November, unable to continue the struggle, the Germans signed an armistice which actually amounted to unconditional surrender. The long war had ended, and a sombre, shattered world turned to the problems of peace.

• The Peace: Optimism and Disillusion

More than ten million men were killed in battle during the four years of World War I and some thirty million more were wounded, many maimed for life. Countless others died of causes indirectly related to the war. The war had not only ravaged the populations of Europe – devoured its youth and consumed its future statesmen – it had caused enormous financial and economic damage. In France alone more than seven million acres of farmland were so devastated that for years they were lost to agriculture. Thousands of factories and mines were completely destroyed all over Europe, and with them raw materials, consumer goods and potential jobs. The psychic damage suffered by populations which had endured starvation and dietary deficiency diseases cannot be measured.

The intensity and destructiveness of the war had inflamed the passions not only of the leaders of the belligerent nations, but of all members of their populations, and when the guns stopped, such passions did not abate. The desire to punish the defeated powers made peacemaking difficult and the German assumption that Wilson's idealistic Fourteen Points would be the basis of the peace compounded the difficulties of creating a settlement which would satisfy anyone.

Negotiations for the treaties which ended World War I were conducted in Paris in 1919 (the victorious Allies refused to permit representatives of the defeated powers to attend). The English and French delegations, headed by Prime Minister David Lloyd George and Premier Georges Clemenceau, were determined to command harsher peace terms than Woodrow Wilson had outlined. Wilson, who wanted above all to establish a League of Nations that would arbitrate international disputes and prevent future wars, was forced to compromise most of his principles to the ambitions of the European powers and to France's demands for security against another German invasion. The resulting settlement did establish a League of Nations, an international body with little real authority and further weakened by the fact that the United States refused to join. The settlement also promulgated a series of treaties which tried to provide self-determination for Europeans, with the glaring exception of Germans.

The Treaty of Versailles, forced on the defeated Germans, created deep and lasting bitterness in Germany because it refused self-determination to 60,000,000 Germans. The majority wished to be joined in a single unified German state, but were kept divided in Germany and Austria, with large minorities in Czechoslovakia and the free city of Danzig. Germany was compelled to return Alsace-Lorraine to France, to cede to Poland territories taken from her in the eighteenth century and, in order to give Poland access to the sea, to relinquish the area of the Polish corridor, which meant dividing Germany into two parts. The Treaty took all of Germany's colonies from her. It curtailed Germany's armed power – severely restricted the size of her army, disbanded the navy, and forbade rearmament. But the most severe blow to German national pride was

Article 231, which forced Germany to accept full responsibility for the war. The "War Guilt Clause" also meant that Germany had to agree to repay the full cost of the war — an economic penalty that Germany, weakened by the war and by her territorial and industrial losses, would find impossible to bear. Moreover, the total amount of the reparations was left unspecified. The German government recognized the injustice of the assertion that Germany alone was responsible for the outbreak of war in 1914, but her representatives accepted the terms of the Treaty of Versailles because they had no choice. The German people never accepted it — they sustained a deep and lasting resentment of its terms.

With the exception of the German provisions, the Versailles Peace Treaty, although not the settlement Wilson had envisioned, reflected reasonably accurately his ideals, as did the treaties with the other defeated states — the Treaty of Saint Germain with Austria, the Treaty of Neuilly with Bulgaria, and the Treaty of Trianon with Hungary. The Austro-Hungarian Empire was shattered into a number of new sovereign nations — Czechoslovakia, Hungary, and Yugoslavia, with Poland, Estonia, Latvia, and Lithuania carved out of former Russian territory (most of these new states were to survive autonomously for less than a generation). The Paris peace settlement, conceived in idealism but born in compromise, did not provide stability in Europe. Instead, it contributed to the chaos which not only prevented security, but prepared the breeding ground for new and not too distant conflicts.

• Revolution in Russia

Of all the European powers embroiled in World War I, the most backward — politically, socially, and economically — was Russia. All authority rested in the hands of the Tsar, Nicholas II, a weak and vacillating individual who could not wield power effectively. Russia had a parliamentary body, the Duma, created in 1906, but such an infant legislature had neither the experience nor the authority to force Nicholas II to make needed social and economic reforms. Russia needed munitions plants, railroads, a modern system of food supply and distribution, an improvement in working conditions, education, and justice, but her government blindly ignored the need for change.

Despite increasing dissatisfaction, however, the Russian people had responded to the war. Some 15,000,000 men were called to the colors and when the first year was over, some 4,000,000 were casualties. During the early months the Russian army fired more shells every day than Russian

Europe-1923

TERRITORIES LOST
By Germany
By Austria-Hungary
By Russia
By Bulgaria

① EUPEN-MALMÉDY
② RHINELAND. ZONE OF ALLIED MILITARY OCCUPATION
③ SAAR-REGION, UNDER LEAGUE OF NATIONS

munitions factories could produce in three months. The army was so poorly equipped that at times the soldiers in the trenches faced the Germans with only one man in three holding a rifle. As the shortages of munitions and food, gross disorganization and lack of leadership became clearer to the soldiers and to the public, the demand for reform increased.

In March, 1917 workers struck a factory in the capital city, Petrograd, and the hungry and angry workers of most of the other factories in the city joined them in bread riots and violence. Troops sent to shoot down the rioters chose instead to join them, and within a few days the city was paralyzed. The movement spread to other parts of Russia, and still the Tsar's government proved ineffective. Before the month was out the Duma appointed a Provisional Government to function as Russia's executive power, and the Tsar abdicated. The Provisional Government and the Duma represented the moderate middle classes, and it appeared for the moment that they could achieve a political revolution which would place them in power without any danger of a really violent social revolution. They intended to carry on the war, write a liberal constitution, and even to provide for a major land reform, but the revolutionary Social Democrats (Marxists) were determined to create a complete social and economic revolution. They organized soviets (committees) all over the country to provide a broad base among the people and prepared to force radical change.

The problems besetting the Provisional Government multiplied in April when Vladimir Ilyich Ulianov (Lenin) returned to Russia from exile in Switzerland. Lenin, a professional revolutionary since the 1880's, had recognized at once the possibility of turning the situation to the advantage of his party, the Social Democrats, and immediately upon his arrival in Russia he attracted a large following. His inflammatory speeches and his slogans, "Land, peace, bread" promised the people exactly what they craved and had a wide appeal to the masses who were desperate for a resolution of the crisis.

During the summer of 1917 while the Germans marched into Russia, starvation and hunger increased, and the revolutionaries demanded that all power be handed over to the soviets. The Provisional Government proved unable to provide adequate leadership, and by November Lenin and his colleagues felt that they had gained enough support to challenge the Provisional Government. In a few hours the Bolsheviks, with army support, successfully accomplished a take-over which placed Lenin and the Bolsheviks in control of all key positions in the government.

• War Communism

Lenin immediately tried to put the ideas of Karl Marx into effect throughout Russia. He nationalized (seized into government ownership) almost all private property, completely abolishing private ownership of land, and expropriated all wealth. "War Communism," this attempt to transform without delay the national economy, caused widespread poverty and hunger, maddened the peasants, who resented having to turn their crops over to the government without getting money in return, and nearly destroyed the Russian people. At the same time Lenin concluded a humiliating peace with Germany. The Treaty of Brest-Litovsk, signed in March, 1918, ceded to the Germans nearly one-third of Russia's population, 1,300,000 square miles of territory, 80 percent of her iron and 90 percent of her coal — vital resources for industrialization. The treaty fanned hatred of Lenin's regime to violence.

Opponents of the new regime, calling themselves "White Russians," as opposed to the "Red Bolsheviks," used the bitterness generated by War Communism to organize a counter-revolutionary movement, and civil war broke out between the "Whites" and the "Reds," which lasted until 1920 – the bloodiest phase of the revolution. Millions, including the Tsar and all his family, died in the conflict – victims of terror perpetrated by both sides.

During the same period Russia faced the shock of foreign invasion. Troops from the United States, England, France, and Japan entered various areas of Russia in support of the anti-Bolshevik forces. The foreign invaders and the Whites never developed a cohesive alliance, however, and the foreign intervention aroused Russian nationalism. Many Russians who would not otherwise have supported the Bolsheviks fled into their ranks to fight the foreigners. Using thousands of former Tsarist Army officers, Leon Trotsky, as Minister of War, organized and trained a 3,000,000 man army and defeated both the Whites and the occupying forces.

● The New Economic Policy

World war, revolution, civil war, and invasion – all these between 1914 and 1921 – proved terribly destructive to the Russian people and their economy. When Lenin imposed War Communism, the system broke down – the peasants refused to turn their produce over to the state without payment, workers resented their conscript status, the new managers proved incompetent. Famine resulted and incalculable suffering turned the people away from the new experiment – between 1914 and 1921 some 28,000,000 Russians died. In order to regain the support of peasants and workers and to get the economy moving, the Bolsheviks retreated toward capitalism. In 1921 Lenin introduced the New Economic Policy (NEP) which lasted until 1928. Under the NEP the peasants paid a fixed tax, then were free to sell any surplus produce on the open market. Private property was re-instituted, small factories and businesses were returned to private management, while the government kept control of heavy industry, banking, transportation, and foreign trade. The NEP proved effective and by 1927 Russia had again reached pre-war levels in industrial production, although agricultural production remained about one-fourth lower than it had been in 1913.

In 1922 Lenin suffered the first of a series of crippling strokes which caused his death in 1924. His illness set off a gigantic power struggle for his position between Leon Trotsky and Joseph Stalin. Trotsky had strong support because he had organized the Red Army and achieved the victory over the Whites and the invading foreigners. He agreed with Marx and Lenin that socialism could not survive in Russia unless the socialist revolution occurred elsewhere. Stalin's power rested on his position as Secretary of the Party, which permitted him to put his own followers into key positions throughout the country. He had rejected hope of immediate world revolution, and believed that Russia must concentrate on establishing "socialism in one country." When Russia had achieved that, she would be in a position to lead and direct the world revolution as the proletariat of other countries proved ready to revolt. Gradually Stalin's control over the Party apparatus (he became Chairman of the Politburo) gave him the victory in the power struggle, and Trotsky was expelled from Russia. He was assassinated in Mexico in 1940.

After defeating Trotsky, Stalin consolidated his iron grip on the Communist Party machinery; only members of the Communist Party could hold any position of leadership or authority. The Party represented only a small percentage of the Russian population (about one percent), but its pyramidal structure penetrated down to the village level, controlling all institutions and dictating all policy. Whoever controlled the Party controlled Russia. Stalin gained total control and by 1930 forced out all opposition and filled the Party with his followers. Once he had assured his personal rule, Stalin was able to turn his attention to creating the socialist state. His ruthless pursuit of the total destruction of all vestiges of capitalism and simultaneous rapid industrialization in Russia meant further misery for the Russian people, and even greater loss of any liberties they had once dreamed of attaining.

• Fascism in Italy

Russia's feeble attempt at democracy had ended in failure. Italy was the next nation to choose totalitarianism. Economically and politically far less advanced than the other western nations, Italy could not overcome the chaos and confusion of the post-war world. Within four years after the cessation of hostilities, Italy, like Russia, had moved to a dictatorship. But Italy chose another type of totalitarian state — a dictatorship of the right. Whereas the Bolsheviks had attempted to establish a socialist utopia patterned on Marxist ideas, the Italians clung fiercely to capitalist ideology, carrying nineteenth-century, middle-class goals to a warped and politically unrecognizable extreme.

Although Italy had fought on the side of the victorious Allies, her gains were small, and many people believed that the western powers had betrayed her. The Italian government had made no real effort to pay for the war — Italy's economy was far too poor, and the Allies had loaned her vast sums. With peace, the government faced an enormous debt and a serious inflation. These economic ills weighed most heavily on those segments of the population who could least afford it — the middle and lower classes. With industry reconverting from wartime to peacetime manufacture, and agriculture retarded by an archaic and inequitable land distribution, jobs were scarce. Soldiers returning home discovered that society could not honor them — it could not even provide them with a living. Unemployment reached staggering proportions.

Those who had jobs were little more satisfied with conditions than those who had none. The failure of the government to fulfill wartime promises of land redistribution and industrial reform created intense frustration in both the rural and urban working classes. Many of the peasants, in bloody rural rebellions, simply seized the land they had expected to acquire. At the same time city workers began a series of violent strikes to stress their loss of faith in the government and to insist on immediate redress of grievances. Lawlessness, aggravated by brigandage, already an Italian tradition, became a vicious counterpart to government in many areas — sometimes whole towns defied the forces of law and order. The success of the Bolsheviks in Russia, the loud-mouthed rhetoric of the small number of communists in Italy, and the chaotic government combined to convince the aristocratic and upper-middle classes that their entire way of life faced extinction. The threat was more imagined than real, but the established classes sought to protect their privileged position and bring order to the nation.

None of these conditions need have been fatal, but the government failed. The political parties fought each other rather than cooperate to solve problems. The Christian Democrats opposed the Socialists, who hated the Liberals' resistance to any government interference in the economy. The entire political system simply incapacitated itself while events moved beyond its control. When unemployment rose, the government did nothing; when gangs of thugs, cut-throats, and brigands terrorized towns and country-side until no one was safe, the government followed a policy of strict non-intervention; when the Treaty of Versailles failed to provide vast additions to Italy's territory, the government sulked. Alienation grew in every class of society. The upper middle classes, wealthy landowners, and industrialists began seeking a strong man to protect their property. The frustrated nationalists, who had pushed Italy into the war, sought a leader who would act to redeem the national honor. Returned veterans looked for one of their own to provide them jobs. The peasants and the workers clamored for peace, security, and economic stability. All of these dissident factions found the leadership they sought in a new faction, the Fascists, whose violence masqueraded as strength. Their founder and creator would, by 1928, become the undisputed leader of Italy — the strong man everyone wanted. His name was Benito Mussolini.

● The Rise of the Fascist Party

In 1919 Mussolini organized the first *fasci di combattimento* — combat groups — of unhappy and discontented citizens. The Fascists, as they became known, capitalized on the dissatisfactions of all the various segments of the Italian population. A small faction in 1919, by 1920 they numbered 30,000; by 1921, nearly 300,000. They began to attract to their ranks representatives of the upper classes and even had adherents in the Italian aristocracy. Government and propertied classes turned to Mussolini, this man of action, who claimed he could protect them from the danger of Bolshevism, and the other classes approved of action rather than the "do-nothing" policies of the existing government. With the consent of the army, the police, and the law courts, Mussolini and his "Black Shirts" — Fascist troops — began a genuine reign of terror against the only groups which showed any inclination to oppose him, the Socialists and Christian Democrats. Labor union offices were burned, newspaper presses destroyed, socialist party headquarters demolished. Anti-Fascists were beaten, had castor oil poured down their throats, their teeth pulled with pliers — many were openly murdered. During 1921 and 1922 the Fascists killed hundreds of people with the active and passive support of those who were supposed to preserve law and order.

Mussolini was elected to Parliament in 1921, along with many of his followers, and by 1922 had enlisted the tacit sympathy of the monarchy and the church. In October, therefore, when the Trade Unions called a General Strike, Mussolini and his Black Shirts swarmed into Rome — the riot later became famous as the "March on Rome" — and the King invited Mussolini to form a cabinet. As Prime Minister, Mussolini formed a coalition government (the Fascists still did not command a majority in the legislature) and then, cloaking his tactics in legality, used his position to gain control of the entire governmental structure. By changing the electoral laws and continuing the terror, the Fascists gained a clear majority in both houses of the legislature. Mussolini demanded and received dictatorial powers, imposed a rigid censorship, and abolished all opposition parties, making the Fascists the only "legal" political party in Italy. Proclaiming himself the *Duce* (Leader), Mussolini rapidly tightened his control of the Italian state until, by 1928, he had completely reorganized the Italian political system.

• The Fascist State

Fascism had no well-thought-out doctrines, no clear ideology. It developed according to the needs of the moment, distinguished, in the beginning, only by its reactionary policies and its determination to achieve power. As it developed, though, patterns began to emerge. It glorified the state above all else — the individual had no significance and no rights except to advance the glory of the state. Fascism therefore denied completely the western concepts of individual freedom and dignity, subordinating the individual to the needs of the state. Along with liberalism and democracy, it vehemently rejected socialism and the economic doctrines of communism. Although Mussolini subjected every aspect of society — politics, economics and cultural life — to a strict authoritarian control, allowing no opposition of any sort, he maintained a state-dominated capitalism. Fascism, then, as developed by Mussolini, became a totalitarian state system which ruthlessly suppressed dissent, glorified nationalism and the nation-state, and adhered rigidly to private (but not free) enterprise and profit. The leadership principle became an essential element of Fascism. Mussolini — the *Duce* — assumed almost mystical leadership over the nation, possessing an emotional and irrational grip over the people. He required total and unquestioning obedience from everyone in Italy — "You must obey because you must."

At first Mussolini retained the appearances of the established Italian political system. Instead of immediately destroying parliamentary institutions, he allowed them to remain in existence but, by filling the cabinet and the legislature with party affiliates, transformed them into sycophantic organizations whose only function was to applaud Mussolini and his policies. Even the King and the Church condoned his usurpation of power. The King remained Monarch, but retained no power or authority — he did whatever Mussolini told him to do. In 1929 Mussolini signed the Lateran Treaty with the Pope, in which Church and State formally recognized each other. Mussolini granted the Church concessions regarding education and marriage law, and the Pope declared that Catholics could in good conscience support Mussolini.

After Mussolini had subjugated the Monarchy, the Church, the Legislature, the Courts and the law enforcement agencies, he began a reorganization of the economy. The Corporate State, the complex economic and political system Mussolini created, was primarily an elaborate justification for economic dominance by the large landowners and wealthy industrialists. In 1925 Mussolini and the Italian industrialists sealed a mutually advantageous pact, the Palazzo Vidoni Agreement, which provided for a highly privileged position for organized industry in return for industry's full support of Mussolini. Mussolini subjugated labor by replacing the old labor unions with Fascist Labor Unions, the only organizations with the right to establish wages, working conditions, and contracts.

Economic and political regimentation, despite the brutality with which it was imposed, did bring order to the former turmoil in Italy and enlisted support for the regime from the lower and middle classes. Moreover, Mussolini silenced any protests which might have arisen by launching an ostentatious program of public works intended to display Italy's prosperity. He built roads, grand new public buildings, improved transportation facilities, and brought water and electricity to rural villages which had never had them before. He encouraged trade, drained marshes and swamps, reclaimed formerly useless land, and subsidized public health programs. At the same time, he staged impressive public spectacles, parades, and party rallies to stir the emotions and the enthusiasm of the population. His propaganda agencies and his censorship program controlled every possible vehicle of influence, and publicized Mussolini and the Fascists. Textbooks, literature, the stage, movies, radio – all proclaimed the glories of Fascism. All the while, the Secret Police assured that no one voiced dissent or even questioned national policy. By 1938 Fascism seemed to have not just the support but the acclaim of every segment of the Italian population. Many thought that Italy had never been as well-run or as prosperous as under Mussolini. Liberty was forgotten – and Fascist propaganda succeeded in convincing the majority of Italians that liberty was not only unimportant, but really undesirable.

Mussolini's glorification of nationalism and his exaltation of the state meant a new surge of imperialism and militarism – expansion by military might of the Italian state. Spurred on by those dissatisfied nationalists hungry for territorial acquisition, Mussolini undertook a policy of military aggression aimed at making Italy the dominant nation in the Mediterranean. Although he did not openly break with the League of Nations, he despised it, and ignored the League's condemnation of his actions when he brazenly and without justification attempted to seize Ethiopia in 1935. In 1936 he violated League neutrality by openly aiding the Franco faction in the Spanish Civil War. After the Nazis attained power in Germany, Mussolini's aggressive foreign policy, which had alienated him from the western European nations, led him into an alliance with Hitler, his Fascist neighbor. Although Mussolini never quite trusted Hitler, both the imperialistic foreign policy and the domestic policies he had launched forced him into tighter and tighter friendship with Germany. The liaison was an extremely dangerous one for Mussolini — ultimately it would prove fatal both to the *Duce* and to the Fascist regime he had constructed.

● The Weimar Republic

The First World War had brought not only defeat but internal chaos to Germany. The long-suffering German people had never been informed of the impending disaster — they were led to believe, until the very end, that Germany was conquering the Allies. At the end of September, 1918, the German Army High Command suddenly and without prior warning informed the Kaiser that an armistice must be arranged without delay, and that the authoritarian government should be changed into a more constitutional and liberal structure to broaden popular support for the Emperor's regime. Prince Max of Baden, a member of the royal family and a liberal statesman, therefore formed a coalition government which had the support of the Social Democratic Party, the largest political party in Germany. As the negotiations for an armistice continued, President Woodrow Wilson made it quite clear that the war would continue until the Kaiser abdicated. The German people, stunned at the sudden reversal of everything they had been told, wanted peace more than anything and believed that only the Kaiser's refusal to abdicate prevented peace. Public discontent intensified and quickly reached a revolutionary stage. When the Naval officers ordered the German fleet to put to sea, the sailors mutinied. At the same time rebellion flared in other portions of Germany. Popular dissatisfaction forced even the Social Democrats, although members of the coalition government, to support the plans for a general strike in favor of abdication. As the rebellion spread, the Kaiser abdicated. Prince Max then handed the reins of government over to Friedrich Ebert, the leader of the Social Democratic Party. Ebert accepted power on the firm promise that he would support the existing constitution.

Conditions throughout Germany, and particularly in Berlin, however, forced the Social Democrats to move toward a democratic republic in order to maintain popular support. Ebert therefore ordered the election of a constituent assembly to draw up a constitution, with all Germans over twenty years of age eligible to vote. Before the election, however, a group of revolutionaries called Spartacists tried to establish by violence a communist government which would have changed the entire social structure of Germany and given power to the working classes. In order to prevent such radical change, the Social Democratic government turned to the old Army under Gustav Noske, self-styled "Bloodhound of the Revolution," who brutally wiped out the uprising.

In southern Germany, Bavaria experienced a particularly brutal civil war during the Spring of 1919 and hundreds of people died in Munich. The defeat of the communists, however, contributed to the development of powerful right-wing organizations which claimed that the Jews were responsible for the attempt to establish a communist government in Munich and in Bavaria. The Social Democratic government was finally victorious over the rebels all over Germany, but only after more than 1,000 people had been killed.

These events of 1918 and 1919 have been called "the German Revolution." The "revolution" was, rather, an attempt to preserve exactly those institutions -- the Monarchy, the Army, and the social structure -- which a genuine revolution would have destroyed. The changes which had occurred in Germany had not basically altered German society. After 1919 Germany had a new and more democratic government in place of the old authoritatian empire. But democracy in Germany was only superficial. It was tolerated by the ruling classes only to defeat the clamor for more extreme change and in the hope of achieving more lenient treatment from the Allies.

On January 19, 1919, elections were held for a National Assembly which met at Weimar on February 6, a coalition of the major political parties in Germany. By the middle of the year the Assembly had provided the legal establishment of the Weimar Republic resting on the people, and operating under the democratic Weimar Constitution. The new Constitution provided for a president to be elected by the people for a seven-year term. Article 48 granted the president the power to govern by decree in the event of a sudden crisis which threatened the republic. Legislative power was vested in a Reichstag, to be elected by universal suffrage, and a Reichsrat, representing the states. A cabinet, headed by a chancellor, was responsible only to the Reichstag.

• Problems Facing the New Republic

From its inception the Weimar Republic faced nearly insurmountable problems. The Allied Powers forced the new government to sign the dictated Treaty of Versailles with its historically false and psychologically unsound clause (Article 231) concerning Germany's sole guilt in causing the war. Resting on that article were the reparations clauses, which stated that Germany must pay the total costs of the war to the victors. All Germans, from extreme left to extreme right, united in bitter opposition to the terms of the treaty. The Chancellor, Philip Scheidemann, and his cabinet resigned rather than sign it. But it had to be signed; the only alternative was military occupation by the victorious troops of the Allied Powers. Nevertheless, the German people refused to accept that reality — they felt that in accepting the treaty the new Government had betrayed the German nation, that Germany had been "stabbed in the back," a constantly repeated phrase. From this time forward far too many Germans accepted the myths constantly dinned into all German ears, that the "November Criminals," the Weimar Constitution, the democrats, and the Jews were responsible for the hated treaty.

The Republic was blamed, too, for the failure to annex German Austria. As the old Habsburg Empire broke into its component national entities, the German portion declared itself part of Greater Germany and requested that the new Weimar government accept it. But the Allies refused to agree to the union of Germany and Austria on the ground that it would be a violation of the Treaty of Versailles. The Allies, and France in particular, feared a large, economically strong German state.

Economic problems of vast proportions plagued the Weimar government. The Reparations Commission immediately took all of Germany's gold reserves and then began to confiscate her capital goods, that is, those items which produce wealth. Specifically, it seized the merchant marine, the fishing fleet, entire machine shops, locomotives, railroad cars, trucks, and any other facilities which could be used to produce goods. Germany thus had to pay an enormous debt, without any of the means necessary to acquire the capital to pay it.

At the beginning of the war the value of the German mark was approximately 25 cents in American currency — four to the dollar. Naturally there had been inflation during the war — there has never been a war without inflation. But the loss of the war and the removal of the gold backing of paper currency inflated the mark to sixty-two to the dollar by May, 1921. At that time the Reparations Commission ordered immediate payment of one billion gold marks and two million per year thereafter, under threat of invasion of the Ruhr Valley, the most highly industrialized area left to Germany. The mark began an immediate slide in value. By June, 1922, scarcely a year later, the situation had deteriorated to such an extent that Germany asked for a moratorium, suggesting that the Allies were killing the goose which laid the golden egg. While England showed signs of agreement, France flatly refused, arguing that Germany really could pay the full amount, that she simply was not trying. Unless Germany paid in full and on time, France insisted that she would occupy the Ruhr and force payment. When this threat failed to produce the desired results, the French moved into the Ruhr area in January, 1923. This step caused more bitterness and hatred in Germany than the entire four years of actual warfare and completed the destruction of the currency. By November 15, 1923, $1.00 would buy 4,200,000,000,000 marks. Some 2,000 printing presses worked twenty-four hours a day stamping paper money — a streetcar ticket cost 16,000,000,000 marks and trade was reduced to barter. The inflation shook Germany to her very roots. The lower middle classes were destroyed — their invested savings wiped out, their pensions and government bonds worthless. Unemployment sky-rocketed and soon, in many areas of Germany, three-fourths of the children were suffering from malnutritional diseases and tuberculosis.

Such economic difficulties contributed to the political problems facing the Weimar Republic and many doubted whether the democratic system could survive. As the inflation approached its peak in November, 1923, a right-wing effort was made to overthrow the Republic. A tiny dissident group had formed in Munich immediately after the war, one of many which developed overnight out of the dislocations and distress of the time. Like the others it lacked leadership, followers, or money. But unlike the others, this one came under the leadership of Adolf Hitler, an Austrian German who had moved to Germany shortly before the outbreak of the war, who had served in the German army, and who had elected to remain in Munich after the war. Hitler proved to have a special and hypnotic effect upon those who heard him speak, and by 1923 he had gained almost complete control over the party, which he renamed the National Socialist German Workers Party (Nazi Party). Hitler firmly established the leadership principle — everyone in the party was totally subservient to "Der Führer," the leader of the party. The authoritarian rule which Germans had accepted under the Kaiser was thus reinstituted, but in a harsher and far more dictatorial manner. Neither Hitler nor the Nazi Party had any coherent political philosophy. They were primitive, ardently nationalistic, and passionately anti-semitic. Above all else, they were men of violence and force. The Nazis organized a private army, called the Brown Shirts, which used violence to intimidate not only the Communists and the Jews, the scapegoats of the German populace, but the government officials themselves.

Bread! Depression in Germany in 1924, from a lithograph by Kathe Kollwitz. Courtesy, Museum of Fine Arts, Boston.

With the support of one of Germany's World War heroes, General Erich von Ludendorff, Hitler and the Nazis attempted to overthrow the government in the famous beer-hall *putsch* in November, 1923. The effort failed, primarily because of lack of preparation, and Hitler was convicted of treason and imprisoned in Landsberg Castle, where he dictated *Mein Kampf* (My Struggle). In this work the Nazi leader outlined the propaganda techniques which would play a powerful role in bringing him to power in 1933, and laid down the outlines of his future aggression and his justification for it. At the same time he made his decision to come to power by legal means, operating at least theoretically within the framework of the Weimar Constitution. This would require careful organization. Hitler had learned from the failure of the Munich *putsch* — he would not make the same mistakes again.

By firm discipline and the introduction of a new currency called the *Rentenmark,* the Weimar Republic pulled out of the inflation and put an end to the internal rebellion. The Allies cooperated, with the Dawes Plan of 1924, which provided for loans from Allied governments to help reestablish German industry and trade. Private capital began to flow into Germany and Germany regained her economic balance — by 1929 her industrial production exceeded that of 1914.

Just when the German people were beginning to feel safe again, the Wall Street Crash in October, 1929 in the United States began the Great Depression which quickly spread to Europe, affecting all the industrialized nations. The short-term credits which had been the foundation of German economic recovery were recalled and within six months the German banks began to fail. By 1931, 17,000 companies had gone bankrupt; during the following year bankruptcies reached the rate of 3,000 per month. Unemployment reached 6,000,000 and many of those who had jobs worked only part-time. At one time, late in 1932, 96 percent of all people who had been employed in the building trades were out of work. The German people once again faced economic collapse. Those classes hardest hit in the inflation of 1923 were now wiped out by the depression. Politics polarized — the moderate political parties lost their support to the extreme parties of both the right and the left. In the September, 1930 election the Communists picked up 77 seats in the Reichstag while the most extreme right-wing party, the Nazis, increased from 12 Reichstag seats to 107 and became the second strongest party in the Reichstag. The parties refused to form an effective coalition which could gain a majority in the legislature, creating extreme political instability. Article 48 — the emergency decree clause — now came into regular use, not for the purpose intended in the constitution, but because of the failure of a majority. In 1932 the Reichstag passed only five laws during the entire year, but the President issued 59 decrees under Article 48. The legislature had ceased to function, and German democracy, ill and weak from birth, died.

- ## The Western Democracies in the Post-War World

England and France had plunged into the First World War without clearly formulated goals or aims. But, before the end, the war became, in the minds of the populations of the western democracies, a fight for democracy against German autocracy. As the devastations of industrial warfare were slowly realized, it became something else as well — a war to end all war. But the savage recriminations between nations continued after the war, resulting in an unjust and vindictive peace settlement. The realization that the war had not created a better world, indeed, had left a heritage of economic and political turmoil affecting all of Europe, created intense disappointment in the West. The European nations which had entered the twentieth century with unbounded optimism, faced the 1920's in a mood of disillusion and despair. Politically and economically they clung to patterns which were time-tried and tested, fearful that experimentation would open the doors to anarchy and revolutions of the kind wracking Eastern Europe. Socially and culturally they abandoned tradition with an almost frenzied fervor.

The 1920's in America and western Europe have been variously described as "the Jazz Age," "the Long Week-end," or "the Lost Generation." Certainly they were years of rapid bewildering social change. Revolutions in transportation, social customs, dress and entertainment transformed the outward pattern of life. Four years of living face-to-face with imminent death were followed by the threat of death from peace-time disease (the flu epidemic of 1918-1919 killed twenty-seven million people in the world — in England alone 200,000 died). The people of the western democracies sought escape from misery by plunging into materialistic indulgence.

War had reinforced strains of doubt beginning to surface in the pre-war decade. Sigmund Freud's theories of the subconscious, known only to the intellectual elite before 1914, now filtered down to the general public and became a popular topic of conversation. Freud's ideas challenged accepted modes of sexual behavior and contributed to a more relaxed moral code, as well as striking a severe blow against the concept that man is a rational being.

Art, music, poetry, and literature mirrored the confusions of the post-war world. Traditional representative art, which depicted a stable, orderly world, was engulfed by the new abstract schools of Cubism, Surrealism, and Expressionism which shattered space and portrayed a fragmented, chaotic universe. Picasso, the foremost painter of the age, led the way in the artistic exploration of modern culture. The Surrealists, like

Salvador Dali and Jean Cocteau, exhibited nightmarish canvasses proclaiming the irrationality of modern man.

Poets articulated the moral despair of the time — T. S. Eliot's *The Waste Land* and *The Hollow Men* described a defeated world peopled with paralyzed, defeated men. Free experimentation with new techniques characterized music and the theatre as well. "Modern" music, to many ears, sounded like the modern world — all dissonance and discord. All the arts reflected the complexities and the bewilderment, the lack of guidelines and the fragmentation of life in the twentieth century.

Yet, along with the rejection of the older moral and social values, there was a simultaneous reassertion of political and economic values. The victory of the Bolshevik regime in Russia powerfully strengthened the conviction, in England, France and the United States, that institutions should not be changed. The western Establishments became quickly convinced that the greatest danger of all was social revolution — that social change would ultimately bring communist revolution.

But the lower classes had discovered their potential during the war, when, through the attrition of upper-class leadership by mass slaughter, officers and government officials had to be drawn from the lower classes. Death had its own equalizing effects. When the soldiers returned home after four years of dreaming of a better life (and propaganda had encouraged those dreams), they did not return easily and quietly to their previous subservience. Demobilization created enormous social tensions, as men returned home to discover that the old class structures still prevailed, and, frequently, that jobs were not available. The result was seething restlessness in the lower classes. During the war women had been employed in all the western democracies in jobs which had formerly been reserved for men. When the men returned to the work force, women were thrown back into their traditional roles. They did not take lightly to the idea of returning to the fireside. In the years following the war women contributed to the social unrest that threatened security by their continuing refusal to be put "back in their place."

In England, in France, and in the United States the social repercussions of the war lasted long into the peace. As the democracies entered the new decade each was faced with social tumult that produced fear and insecurity, and an accompanying nostalgia for the past. Every new demand from any segment of the population, whether it was the right to vote by women, better pay for work, improved working or housing conditions, appeared to the upper class establishments as a dire attack on everything of value in the culture of the "golden years" before the war.

All of the democracies experienced serious economic problems after the war. Each faced rising prices, reconversion of industry to peacetime production, rising unemployment, large public debts and shrinking international trade. During the war, England, France, and the United States had resorted to governmental regulation of the economy and central planning to boost the war effort. Instead of retaining planning to solve the economic dislocations of the peace, each nation rapidly rejected war-time controls. Their adherence to limited government intervention failed to resolve the problems of peace. As economic structures broke down, unrest in the populations increased, along with more and more strident demands for change.

• England

Over two million British citizens were killed or wounded on the battlefields of World War I. Moreover, England had invested forty-four billion dollars in the war effort — increasing her national debt ten times over pre-war levels. Although her property damage was not nearly as great as that of Germany and France, her economic difficulties were severe. In the years immediately following the war the Labour Party, born in 1906, attracted enough electoral support to become the largest opposition party in the House of Commons. The Labour Party, after 1918 a self-proclaimed socialist party, demanded radical methods of attacking economic troubles, such as nationalization of industry. Conservatives and the old Liberal Party viewed such drastic measures with great antipathy, but were unable to combat Labour's growing attraction to workers, farmers, trade-unionists, and those of the middle and upper classes who were insistent on economic reform.

Immediately after the war a Liberal-Conservative Coalition government, under the leadership of David Lloyd-George, tackled the initial problems of the peace. By 1921, however, its efforts had proved so disappointing that the coalition collapsed. In the 1922 election Liberals and Conservatives both campaigned on fears of the new Labour Party and the dangers of Bolshevism. So real was the fear, although of course not the reality, that even Labour moderated its economic proposals and vehemently denied any ties to communism. The emotional issue, however, catapulted the Conservatives into power under Bonar Law. Law was already seriously ill with the cancer which would kill him in 1923 and proved an ineffectual leader in a time of mounting discontent. When his illness forced his resignation in 1923, the King called on Stanley Baldwin to form a government. Baldwin, who would be a dominant British political figure during the crucial decades between the wars, was an old-line Conservative who viewed the rise of Labour as an unmitigated disaster for England. A rather apathetic individual whose most distinguishing trait was mediocrity, he marshalled the Conservative troops in the fight against change. He offered the electorate empty slogans — "Faith, Hope, Love, and Work" — instead of vigorous solutions. His failure to solve the deep-seated problems facing Great Britain turned voters increasingly in the direction he most feared — to Labour. In 1924 Liberals and Labour aligned against his government and brought it down. For the first time, the King called on the leader of the Labour Party, Ramsay MacDonald, to form a government.

Although conservative Englishmen deplored the move, fearing "the horrors of socialism and confiscation," there was no real danger. Labour's rhetoric was more radical than its sentiments — it was firmly rooted in democracy and enormously susceptible to the blandishments of the middle class. Moreover, since the Party had no clear majority, it had to rely on Liberal support. There were, however, some domestic reforms. Some of the wartime tariffs were abolished. The government provided extended educational opportunities for laboring class children, built new housing at controlled rents for workers, and increased payments for unemployment. But attention rested primarily on foreign, not domestic, policy. Britain, convinced that German economic reconstruction was essential to her own recovery, played a significant role in drafting and supporting the Dawes Plan, which eased the German reparations payments somewhat. At the same time England encouraged France to remove her troops from the Ruhr Valley. MacDonald's determination to settle the international tensions left by the war in order to improve the economic situation at home led him to grant full recognition to Soviet Russia. He also signed treaties providing large loans to Russia because he believed that the Russians would then be enabled to purchase British goods and improve England's lagging export trade. But both Liberals and Conservatives vehemently opposed such close relations with the outlaw communist nation. Fearing Labour's seeming alignment with Bolshevism, they brought down the Labour government with a vote of no confidence. In the resulting election, again under Stanley Baldwin's leadership, the Conservatives campaigned on a program of saving England from Bolshevism and won a clear majority. Thereafter, for several years, the Conservatives maintained almost complete control of the government.

British industry continued to fail miserably to move with the times. Equipment, machinery, and methods, all lagged behind other countries. The dole, unemployment, falling exports — in short, economic ill-health —

endured. Politically, as well, England could not pull out of the doldrums. A weary electorate returned Labour to power in 1929, again with Liberal support. In 1931, however, England was engulfed in the Great Depression and a genuine crisis forced MacDonald's resignation. A "National Government," a coalition of all three major parties, was formed to deal with the situation, and made token efforts to cure England's economic diseases. But British statesmen, no matter what the party stamp, paralyzed by their fear of radical change, could not alter their basic economic assumptions sufficiently to get England back on her feet. Gradually, Conservative domination of the coalition gave way to Conservative control of the political system which endured through the 1930's. England in the 1920's had hesitantly and reluctantly experimented with minor innovation by twice voting Labour into office, but had finally rejected even the desire to try new approaches. Tired and apathetic, England moved into the 1930's with little vigor to fight the challenge of Fascist aggression.

• France

France suffered severe physical and psychic damages during World War I. She put eight million men into uniform and five million were casualties — in a country which already had a low birthrate and in which women outnumbered men by about 2 percent. During the war the population declined by four million; in the civilian population there were one and a half million more deaths than births, and by 1921 France had a female population which exceeded males by 15 percent. More than three quarters of a million buildings had been destroyed, along with roads, bridges, railroads, and mines. The animal population had also sharply declined. Industrial and agricultural production suffered irreparable damage. Almost immediately after the war vast numbers of peasants flocked to the cities and towns and since most had no marketable skills, they joined radical unions which became communist strongholds. The polarization of politics into a loudly protesting left and a sometimes violently defensive right occurred more drastically in France than it did in England.

The government of the Third Republic contained fatal weaknesses. The executive, directly responsible to the legislature, could be turned out of office immediately, as in England, but the legislature was elected for fixed four-year terms. Unlike England, the cabinet could not call a new election to determine the wishes of the population. The existence of over two dozen political parties, no one of which could ever claim a clear majority, worsened the situation. Every cabinet had to be a coalition cabinet, and most did not last long enough to do anything constructive. The governments of France in the years after the war demonstrated extreme instability of leadership, of policy, and vast inefficiency. Between 1919 and 1933 France had twenty-seven different cabinets. The real conduct of affairs was left to civil service officials, who provided the only degree of continuity and stability the system possessed, but who opposed any changes in policy.

The government seemed utterly incapable of solving the problems that rocked France after the war. Almost everyone was imbued with a sick fear of Germany and a determination to insure that Germany would never again invade France as she had in 1870 and 1914. A passion for security gripped Frenchmen and blinded them to the need for reform. This became clear even at the peace conference when it appeared to England and the United States that France wanted to ruin Germany. France wanted reparations, she wanted buffer states, she wanted a strong Poland, and she wanted the colonial empires of Germany and Turkey. But at the same time, Frenchmen needed to relax after the years of terrifying destruction of World War I. Soldiers impatiently awaited demobilization, businessmen wanted relief from taxes, and workingmen wanted to improve their standard of living. France had problems of such enormity even a young, dynamic leadership would have found them overwhelming. Instead, they had to be solved by old men, who faced the twentieth century with fear and trepidation, and with outdated answers.

Rigid enforcement of the Treaty of Versailles took precedence over all else in the immediate post-war years. France's vehement policy of kicking the dead German horse came into direct conflict with England's policy of restoring Germany in order to rebuild the world economy and caused mistrust between the two European nations. The climax of dissension occurred in 1923 when France, under the leadership of the arch-conservative Raymond Poincaré, an aged man with residual hostilities toward Germany from the pre-war period, invaded the Ruhr in an attempt to force full German payment of reparations. The United States and England opposed France, and the French people, bitterly resenting further military expenditures, became increasingly dissatisfied with the government and its policies.

In 1924 Aristide Briand became Premier and for a time succeeded in establishing a more rational foreign policy. Briand believed strongly in reconciliation. Cooperating with Gustav Stresemann, then German Foreign Minister, he ended the French occupation of the Ruhr and concluded the Treaty of Locarno, which initiated a period of reduced international tensions and surface harmony. Briand also recognized the

Soviet government in Russia and regularized French relations with that country.

Briand's domestic policies met with considerably less success, however. The inflationary spiral affecting all of Europe hit France with extraordinary severity. The franc, worth twenty cents before the war, devalued to a low of two cents in 1926. The crisis brought down Briand's government and returned Poincaré to office. Through a new tax program and vigorous economic measures Poincaré managed to stabilize the French currency and prevent disaster. By 1928 the new currency rate was established at just under four cents, or 20 percent of its pre-war value. But the inflation caused wide suffering. Small investors and many moderately prosperous members of the middle-class were wiped out and lost their remaining faith in the government. The very class which had most vigorously supported republican principles and ideals, in their fear of being pushed down into the lower classes, moved sharply to the conservative right and became almost fanatical opponents of any change which seemed to issue from the left.

As the decade of the 1920's neared a close, France faced economic and political tensions of even greater severity than those debilitating England. When depression struck France in 1932, she was already largely immobilized by political and economic dislocation. She would not be able to pull out of the decline, and the international crises of the 1930's would ultimately sound the death knell of the Third Republic.

• The United States

Unlike her European allies or the defeated Central Powers, the United States did not suffer greatly from World War I. She emerged from the war victorious and unhurt, with enormously increased international prestige, undisputed economic leader of the world. After a brief depression in 1921 as war-time economic controls were abandoned and demobilization caused some unemployment and labor unrest, America entered into a period of unrivalled economic growth and expansion. Yet Americans shared the disillusionment that gripped the western world after the war. She had escaped most of the horrors of war and did not want to take on the responsibilities of peace.

Determined not to get involved in any further European conflicts, Americans refused to ratify the Versailles Treaty or to join the League of Nations. In 1920 voters turned Woodrow Wilson and the Democrats out of office, handing the reins of government over to the Republicans, who would keep them for the next twelve years. The Republican candidate, Warren G. Harding, a political unknown with the ability to say absolutely nothing while sounding profound, won a resounding victory in a campaign which pleaded a return to pre-war security. "America's present need," he said, "is not heroics but healing; not nostrums but normalcy; not revolution but restoration; . . . not surgery but serenity."

Normalcy meant complacency. It meant a return to a government policy of allying with big business to remove controls. Corruption, bribery, and attacks on personal liberties marked the Harding administration. Calvin Coolidge's administration which followed continued the patterns established under Harding without the corruption. Coolidge supported business totally, and efforts on the part of labor to improve its position found no sympathy either in the government or the population.

Normalcy also meant intolerance. Fear of change plus social and economic unrest caused a desperate effort to force adherence to traditional values. Hundreds of innocent aliens were deported; the National Origins Act prevented immigration of any but White Anglo-Saxon Protestants (WASPS); and the Ku Klux Klan boasted a membership approaching 5,000,000 across the country. The Eighteenth Amendment made alcohol unconstitutional. New York State's Assembly expelled five properly elected representatives simply because they were socialists, and a Tennessee court convicted a high school teacher for teaching Darwin's theory of evolution.

The United States withdrew from the position of leadership in world affairs which her successful intervention in the war had won. She continued to participate in the attempt to stabilize international relations, however, by encouraging disarmament and combatting militarism. In 1922 at the Washington Conference the United States, China, Japan, and six European nations met to consider naval armaments and the settlement of problems in the Far East. The Conference resulted in an agreement to respect the integrity and territorial independence of China, and it established naval ratios among the world powers intended to prevent any naval armaments race. Significantly, Russia was not invited. In 1926 the American Secretary of State, Frank B. Kellogg, together with Aristide Briand of France submitted to the nations of the world a naive proposal outlawing war as a means of settling international disputes. Twenty-three nations signed the Kellogg-Briand Pact. Throughout the decade the United States worked with England and France to solve the problem of German reparations.

Yet Americans, despite these efforts to encourage world-wide cooperation between nations, shared a growing conviction that the United

States must remain uncontaminated from the virulent diseases striking Europe. Reluctant to face the fact that in the twentieth-century world no nation can remain truly independent, she continued to pursue policies aimed at keeping uninvolved. The immigration restrictions of the 1920's were an expression of defensive American nationalism and growing isolationist sentiment — so were the high protective tariffs enacted at a time most damaging to world trade. Isolationism in the 1920's was not so extreme as it became in the 1930's, but the seeds of America's abdication of responsible leadership were sowed in the post-war decade. And America's failure during those same years to solve her own economic ills, eating away beneath the surface at the foundations of her booming prosperity, was a primary cause of Europe's final collapse.

20

The Lights Finally Go Out: International Anarchy, 1930-1945

IN OCTOBER, 1929 the New York Stock Exchange collapsed. America had experienced stock market declines before, along with economic depressions, but never one of this magnitude. A decade of over-extended credit and complacent confidence that American prosperity was boundless had resulted in an economy that was entirely out of balance. The Stock Market Crash set off the worst depression in United States history. In the twentieth century, with its interdependent industrial economies, the American economic disaster soon affected most of the industrial nations of the world.

By 1931, as Americans withdrew the capital they had invested in Europe and recalled loans at a rapid rate, major European banks began to fail. Because of the crisis the United States agreed to a one-year moratorium on war debts, since the European nations, without the help of American capital, clearly could not pay. But it was too late; the depression had already struck.

- ## The Great Depression and World Repercussions

As the depression spread throughout the world, the major governments took measures which made the situation worse. At a time when an increase in world trade was most needed, governments raised tariffs, introduced quotas, and insisted on economic self-sufficiency. Almost every country instituted "buy-at-home" programs. But the economic crisis was too severe to be easily overcome. And it brought in its wake a wave of radicalism in the lower classes which awakened a fierce reaction to the right, and a renewed faith in authoritarian concepts. The political tensions which had simmered below the surface in the 1920's erupted into full boil in the 1930's — a direct response to the economic collapse.

• The New Deal

In the United States the depression deepened between 1929 and 1932 and the government, handicapped by its conviction that government should not play too direct a role in the economy, seemed incapable of finding a solution. President Herbert Hoover refused to allow direct government relief for the unemployed and insisted that the federal budget must remain balanced. As his correctives proved increasingly ineffectual, Americans began to examine more carefully the concept of government economic controls. The crisis made the public aware that the new industrial society had invalidated the old policies of laissez-faire.

In 1932 Americans voted the Democrats back into office. President Franklin Delano Roosevelt emerged as a dynamic leader who initiated a program of vigorous action which gave the public new hope. His New Deal program aimed at modifying the capitalist system in order to save it. Although they did not immediately conquer all the problems of the depression, within a short time Roosevelt's policies began to rejuvenate the American economy. The success of his program undermined extremism in American politics, and the United States survived the 1930's without the political upheavals the European nations were to experience. The economic crisis had caused Americans to shift slightly to the left — in the direction of greater government control of the economy. Americans did not entirely reject economic liberalism, but realistically accepted the fact that modern economies must be organized.

• England's National Government

In England the Labour Party had come to power just a few months before the Wall Street crash. Despite the radical economic program proposed after 1918, Labour, again led by Ramsay MacDonald, proved to be as reluctant as Herbert Hoover to take vigorous action. MacDonald pursued a policy of retrenchment and, when he refused to increase government aid to the unemployed, his cabinet fell. A National Government, theoretically a coalition of Conservatives, Liberals, and Labour, took its place. By 1932 England had abandoned her long-standing, free trade position, enacted protective tariffs, and joined the other European nations and the United States in an excess of economic nationalism.

By a desperately needed housing program which helped reduce unemployment and by keeping interest rates low so that purchasing power was extended, the National Government created a slight recovery by 1936, but unemployment still remained discouragingly high, and production low. England, typically, managed to muddle through without political crisis. By 1937, as a measure of prosperity returned, it was evident that striking changes in attitude had occurred and the government had entered more strongly into economic regulation. But recovery was slow, and Englishmen, as they increasingly accepted the necessity of centralized economic planning, demanded further extensions of government responsibility. The attitudes which would ultimately initiate the welfare state in England took shape during the depression decade.

● Popular Front in France

The depression hit France somewhat more slowly than the other European states. By 1932, however, the collapse of world markets, falling exports, and the declining tourist trade had pulled France into the economic slump. The conservative orientation of French politicians and the instability of French politics made it exceedingly difficult to cope with the depression. A small, wealthy clique of 200 families controlled most of France's capital, and vehemently resisted rigid governmental controls. The rest of the population feared further devaluation of the franc, and the government resisted deficit spending. Consequently, nothing effective was done to curb the deepening economic decline in a nation which had scarcely recovered from the war.

At the same time France watched with fear and apprehension the rise of the Nazis in Germany. Caught in the conflict between the communist system in Russia and the threatening Fascist systems in Germany and Italy, French policy vacillated, hesitated, and floundered. The economic collapse created a more extreme polarization of political opinion in France than it had in England and the United States, and France struggled through the thirties, rocked from left and right. As the depression dragged on, Frenchmen increasingly sought drastic solutions. Active organizations of the right, such as the reactionary *Action Francaise,* an extremely nationalistic, royalist group, clashed disturbingly with a rapidly solidifying left.

In 1934 a scandal in high government circles demonstrated clearly the malaise affecting French politics. The government was implicated in the murder of Serge Alexandre Stavisky, a financial swindler with numerous connections in government. The government, dominated by the middle-class Radicals, seemed riddled with corruption. Public indignation reached fever pitch and riots broke out nightly.

The cabinet resigned, and was succeeded by a series of weak governments which were utterly incapable of remedying the political or economic situation. The left insisted that France was being run by Fascists; the right declared that the Socialists and Communists were menacing the state. Hitler's successful remilitarization of the Rhineland in 1936 intensified the struggle.

The government's continuing failure to bring stability to France had caused the parties of the left to solidify into a weak union called the Popular Front. Although Socialists and Communists remained bitter enemies, and the moderate-center Radical Party supported the union indecisively, the Popular Front won a clear-cut electoral victory in 1936. For the first time, France had a socialist Premier. Leon Blum was by no means a representative of the radical left, however. He was neither a Marxist nor a revolutionary, but had joined the Socialists out of his conviction that France desperately needed reform.

Under Blum's leadership the government undertook a program of social reform. He ordered the leaders of capital and labor to sit down with him to work out compromises which would modernize France's economic system. The resulting Matignon Agreements laid the foundations for the future welfare state in France. Representatives of the managerial class agreed to the eight-hour day, forty-hour week, minimum wage scale, paid vacations, and the right to collective bargaining. But many employers used every possible method to evade the new regulations.

The Conservatives reacted furiously and "Better Hitler than Blum" became a prominent slogan. The Radical Party, hesitant from the beginning and committed to principles of laissez-faire, pulled out of the coalition, bringing the cabinet down. The Blum government, the only French cabinet in the inter-war period to attempt to come to terms with the modern world, had lasted just over a year. After its fall in 1937 the French people drifted more and more to the right, without vitality or strength, which resulted in their rapid capitulation to Hitler in 1940. Faced with economic crisis, France proved incapable of even the compromises England and the United States had reluctantly accepted. The failure of the French system to adapt to changing times marked the final disintegration of the Third Republic.

● Responses Around the World

All over Europe democracy was in crisis. The depression gave impetus to extremism and violence against which the frail democratic systems established after World War I could not prevail. Socialist parties grew rapidly in response to the obvious failure of the older economic policies to restore prosperity. The left, ordinarily splintered into rival factions, consolidated in an attempt to gain strength through unity. These coalitions of the left – Popular Fronts – gained power only briefly, however. A Popular Front emerged in Spain in 1934 and managed to initiate some reform in that extraordinarily backward state, but the opposition to reform policies was so strong that Spain became embroiled in civil war.

In other areas of Europe the depression undermined confidence in political institutions, causing varying degrees of change. The smaller western nations, Belgium, Switzerland, and the Scandinavian countries, managed to cling to their long-established democratic institutions by accepting the idea of government intervention in the economy and state regulation of business. The newer democracies of eastern Europe, however, moved rapidly toward authoritarianism and dictatorship. In the 1930's dictatorships arose in Yugoslavia, Rumania, Bulgaria, and Albania. Austria attempted to retain a modicum of democracy, but it was shaky at best. Only Czechoslovakia succeeded in preserving a democratic state, but it was constantly threatened by factionalism.

The impact of the depression was not limited to Europe and the United States – the economic collapse sent shock waves around the world. The industrial nations were most directly affected. Between 1918 and 1930 Japan seemed to be moving in the direction of liberalism and parliamentarianism. But the government faced enormous difficulties. Wealth and power were concentrated in the hands of a few individuals reluctant to share it, and western traditions were alien to Japanese culture. In 1931, when Japanese export trade had so sharply declined that the entire economy suffered, extremist elements fatally attacked Japanese democracy. The Prime Minister, Hamaguchi, who had pursued liberal, pacifist policies, was assassinated and in the ensuing crisis the reactionary elements in Japan gained control. The new government was an ultranationalistic, military dictatorship, intent on spreading the "New Order" to all of Asia. That meant expansion of the Japanese state and Japanese domination of the Far East.

• Solutions in Germany

In 1930, as banks and businesses failed, and unemployment climbed above 3,000,000, the German people elected 77 Communists and 107 Nazis to the Reichstag. Since no coalition of parties could be formed to provide majority support for a cabinet, the people accepted a presidential cabinet which ruled by decrees issued under Article 48 of the constitution. The moderate parties permitted the failure of the democratic process because they feared that another election would establish a dictatorship of either the Communists or the Nazis.

The presidential cabinet, however, could not solve the economic and social problems; unemployment continued to rise, going above 6,000,000 in 1932, while the private armies of the Nazi and Communist Parties carried on pitched battles in the streets, and murdered their opponents. Hitler's propaganda machine worked overtime to convince the people of all classes that the Nazis could and would solve all problems and that order and security depended on a Nazi government. In July, 1932 the Nazis elected 230 members to the Reichstag, thus becoming the largest party in Germany.

A small group of men, representing the Army, the aristocracy, big business and the bureaucracy convinced President Hindenburg that Germany faced civil war and Bolshevization unless the Nazis were brought into the government. They believed that they could control Hitler and the Nazis in the cabinet. On January 30, 1933 President Hindenburg appointed Hitler Chancellor, heading a cabinet of Nazis and Nationalists, and within little more than a year Hitler had established a totalitarian dictatorship.

The reasons for the failure of the Weimar Republic are numerous and complex. But the central fact is simply that the democratic process failed in Germany. The events surrounding Hitler's appointment as Chancellor have far less significance than the failure of the democratic leadership throughout the fourteen years of the Republic. Too many Germans opposed the Weimar Republic for too many reasons. The Social Democrats lacked the courage and vision to introduce socialism, and many workers who wanted socialism believed Hitler would establish it. Many leading Nazis before 1933 were genuine socialists, disenchanted with the Social Democrats' failure to live up to their rhetoric. Monarchists opposed the republic without the courage to restore monarchy. Big businessmen opposed the idea of a republic, or the democratic process, and especially of giving any role to the labor unions, but they lacked the ability to suggest any positive alternatives. So with the army, which supported Adolf Hitler, the one man who guaranteed action. Ultimately the Weimar Republic failed because its leaders could not solve the problems which plagued the German people, and thus permitted a drift into demagogic rule.

- ## Totalitarian Germany

From the moment of his appointment as Chancellor, Hitler showed himself to be intensely activist. His was to be a "do-something" regime. In Prussia every office was filled with Nazis and Nazi supporters, and the Brownshirts (the Nazi private army) were deliberately loosed upon any opposition with instructions to shoot left-wing opponents. A reign of terror developed throughout Prussia, and spread into the other German states. In the midst of the disorder Hitler called for another election to the Reichstag, to be held in March, 1933. When, shortly before election day, the Reichstag building burned, the entire Communist Party received the blame, and was outlawed; thousands of Communist and Socialist leaders were arrested, and all left-wing newspapers were banned. On the pretext that the Communists and Socialists had jointly planned a civil war, the government suspended the constitutional guarantees of basic human rights. The Nazis gained several million more votes in this election than they had previously garnered and Hitler now demanded that the Reichstag pass the Enabling Act of March, 1933, to give him dictatorial powers for four years. With the Communist Party outlawed, and with many Social Democrats under arrest, the Reichstag overwhelmingly passed the Enabling Act.

Hitler used his new powers to abolish all political parties except his own, to destroy the separate existence of the individual German states, to wipe out all labor unions, and to bring every single facet of German life under totalitarian Nazi control. In the place of the traditional labor unions the Nazis established the German Labor Front, which incorporated both labor and management in a single organization completely controlled by the party. Thus strikes and lockouts were outlawed. A special law was promulgated which unified party and state and, after President Hindenburg's death in 1934, even the offices of President and Chancellor were merged in the person of Hitler. Schools, newspapers, radio, drama, cinema, every means of communication, came under the control of the Ministry of Propaganda, and many Germans joined in burning outlawed books. All children from the age of ten years were forced into the Hitler Youth to be molded into Nazis.

By June, 1934 Hitler faced the inevitable development in any revolutionary situation — some wanted the revolution to go further, while conservative elements wanted to pause. Hitler moved swiftly. On the Night of the Long Knives, June 30, 1934, his personal henchmen killed off the leadership of the radical wing, and included a number of conservatives to indicate that he would not tolerate opposition from any direction. Hitler announced to the German people that the hundreds who had been slaughtered were killed on his orders, and that he was entitled to administer justice on his own authority. The German state and the German people had been mastered.

• Economic Solutions

Probably none of Hitler's actions would have been sufficient to maintain his control had he not solved many of Germany's more serious problems. When he came to power, almost 4,000,000 Germans were out of work. Hitler set out to bring Germany to full employment, and in this he was largely successful. Vast public works projects employed many men, who then became consumers, priming the economic pump. A highway system, the best in the world at that time, used huge numbers of laborers, as did reforestation projects and the draining of swamps. A housing program reached its peak in 1937 with the construction of more than 300,000 houses, mostly one and two family units, complete with gardens. At the same time organizations such as "Strength Through Joy" provided paid vacations for workers which they could never have dreamed of under earlier regimes. Such tactics helped Germans forget that they were being taxed excessively and that much of the money used for their vacations came from confiscated property of other Germans who languished in concentration camps or who had been killed. By 1936 there was a labor shortage, especially in skilled occupations, and the depression had been solved.

Millions of Germans from every economic and social class in the state actively supported Hitler and the Nazis. Hitler fully understood how to use propaganda to convince the masses that he knew exactly what their needs were and that he was fulfilling them. Those who opposed the new regime ended up in concentration camps or were shot by the Gestapo, the secret police. People were arrested, tortured, and thrown into concentration camps without trials or any semblance of legality. Thus even those who did not actively support Hitler quickly found it expedient to go quietly about their business.

Propaganda hid the fact that the Nazi movement lacked any ideological base. The Nazis were essentially activists, using whatever came to hand in lieu of ideology. After January, 1933 anti-Semitism was consciously developed as part of the Nazi program. By 1935 the Nuremberg Laws proscribed marriages between Jews and Aryans and placed numerous restrictions on their lives. Soon no Jew could be employed in Germany and Jewish children could not attend school with Aryans. But they could not leave Germany without leaving all their property and often had no place to go anyway. By 1938 officially sanctioned pogroms against the Jews were commonplace, and the Nazi government placed a billion-mark fine on the whole Jewish community on the pretext that a Polish Jew had killed a German diplomat in Paris.

After World War II began, it was decided to exterminate all the Jews in Europe. At first the Jews were marched into ditches and shot. Gradually the Germans refined their techniques until they developed gas chambers and crematoria such as those at Auschwitz, where at least 3,000,000 people were slaughtered, all but some 20,000 of them Jews.

• Hitler's Foreign Policy

Part of Hitler's appeal to the German people rested on his foreign ambitions. All Germans could applaud the idea of breaking the chains of the hated Treaty of Versailles. Germany must be rearmed, German territory must be reclaimed, and German people brought back under the protective mantle of the Fatherland. As early as October, 1933 Hitler flamboyantly withdrew Germany from the League of Nations, and pulled out of the Disarmament Conference then going on, on the popular grounds that both these bodies intended to keep Germany disarmed, while other nations rearmed. German industry was given huge government orders for armaments, a road system was designed for military purposes, and in 1935 Hitler announced to the world that he was building an air force and a navy. To provide manpower for them, he reintroduced universal military training and conscription. Conservative economists objected that the armaments projects disrupted the reviving economy, and the generals objected on the grounds that Germany might have to fight a two-front war which she would lose. Hitler responded by establishing a Second Four-Year Plan, designed to place Germany in readiness for war within four years. This move placed effective control over the economy in the hands of the Nazi Party, masterminded by the brilliant Dr. Hjalmar Schacht. Hitler himself directed that Germany was to be completely independent of all foreign powers as soon as possible in all the materials which might be needed for war. The scientific community bent every effort to creating substitutes for those raw materials which Germany lacked. Artificial rubber, synthetic fabrics, plastics, and numerous other developments cut down Germany's need for imports. Having firmly established totalitarian control over Germany, Hitler now prepared for mastery of Europe.

• The Soviet Industrial Revolution

During the 1930's the western nations moved at varying rates of speed toward state controlled economies. The example of the soviet system which had emerged in Russia between 1917 and 1923 served a paradoxical function: ultra-right-wing groups in Germany and Italy had utilized fear of Bolshevism to precipitate the establishment of totalitarian, statist regimes, but the western democracies, equally fearful of Russian Communism, had shied away from further centralization of state power and from much-needed government economic planning. At the same time, all of the European nations isolated Russia from international affairs, and softened their resistance to Fascist aggression. Developments in Russia between 1928 and 1939 gave impetus to each of these reactions.

While Russia had moved to political dictatorship after the Bolshevik revolution, between 1923 and 1928 the Soviet Union had not established a socialist state, although few in the West recognized that fact. The New Economic Policy, instituted after the failure of War Communism, had preserved many elements of capitalism, and retarded progress toward the socialist goal. Under the NEP industrialization had progressed only slowly, and the policy had permitted the growth of the Kulak class – peasants who owned their own land and sold their products on the market, and who vehemently opposed further socialization. The economic agencies of the state did not in reality control the Russian economy.

In 1927 Stalin determined to forcefully establish a pure socialist economy in Russia. His goal was to turn Russia from a backward, rural, agricultural economy with little industry into a highly industrialized state with centralized economic organization and planning, and to wipe out the remains of capitalism, private ownership, and profit. To effect such a transformation, Stalin had to accomplish two formidable tasks: agriculture had to be collectivized – that is, brought under state ownership and control – and industrial facilities had to be built. An economic revolution of such magnitude creates extreme difficulties for a population. But Stalin was not the man to allow humanitarian concerns to deter him. In a period of just ten years, he achieved his economic goals, but at an enormous cost in human misery and suffering.

- **Collectivization of Agriculture**

The collectivization of agriculture and an increase in agricultural production were necessary first steps toward creating the socialist state. Agriculture remained fantastically primitive, with even the best Russian farmers producing only about 15 percent as much as their American counterparts. Earlier efforts to gain the support of the peasants had actually decreased the size of farms, which were far too small to make efficient use of machinery. Russian farmers marketed less than half as much grain in 1928 as they had in 1913. Kulaks often refused to sell their grain at government pegged prices and strenuously resisted attempts to merge their property into large, state-run farms.

The effort to collectivize Russian agriculture turned into a veritable civil war between the middle and upper level of peasants on the one hand and the poorer peasants and the government on the other. Entire Kulak villages were destroyed and the Kulak class was entirely wiped out. In the conflict crops and livestock perished, causing famine and starvation. During the period of enforced collectivization five million Russians died, along with half of all the livestock in the country. Many other peasants were sent to forced labor camps in Siberia, where they were forced to open up new lands to agriculture.

Between 1933 and 1935 a new Russian agricultural system emerged. The collective farms were large estates, averaging well over one thousand acres each, farmed by several families according to central planning. Tractor stations issued heavy equipment to all farms and insured control by refusing it if a farm did not conform to government policies. Individual families were permitted to own only small plots of land for home gardens and livestock for family use. By 1933 more than 50 percent of Russia's agricultural families lived on collective farms, and by 1939, when war interfered with further extension of the program, 95 percent of all Russian agriculture had been collectivized.

- **The Five Year Plans**

The creation of a new industrial society caused as much hardship as had the agricultural revolution. Russia had few skilled laborers and technicians, and had to hire them from the more industrially advanced nations. Furthermore, enormous capital was required to create the bases of an industrialized economy — machines, tools, electrical generating plants, oil refineries and steel mills. Stalin decided to sacrifice housing and consumer goods to the production of the necessary basic elements of the new economy.

In 1928 Russia launched the first of the Five Year Plans, the most massive program of economic restructuring ever undertaken. Under the direction of the *Gosplan,* the state planning agency, the First Five Year Plan, which ran from 1928 to 1933, was succeeded by the Second (1933-1937). World War II prevented completion of the Third.

The Soviet State engaged all of its energies in realizing Stalin's economic goals. Soviet propaganda ceaselessly proclaimed the worthiness of the Five Year Plans. Absenteeism, slow-downs, incompetence – all suddenly became crimes against the state and drew heavy penalties, frequently up to twenty years at hard labor in Siberia. A person convicted of stealing state-owned property could expect the death penalty, no matter how small the value of the stolen object. At the same time, those whose production exceeded the average or who contributed to increasing efficiency received special rewards. Pay was made proportionate to production, and highly efficient teams of workers received the glory and publicity accorded military heroes in war-time.

Measured by industrial achievement, the Five Year Plans were an overwhelming success. Thousands of new factories were built, new agricultural areas opened, new industrial complexes created. In ten years Russia became one of the front-ranking industrial powers in the world. In 1939 only two countries reported greater industrial production than the Soviet Union – the United States and Germany. The cost to the individual had been great, but the response of the Russian people had been surprisingly cooperative; the effectiveness of the propaganda program and the obvious industrial achievements had generated an excitement for the projects and the long-range goals. Simply to be part of such an endeavor attracted many to its support.

• "Socialism in One State"

The consolidation of the Soviet police state ensured cooperation where it did not develop voluntarily. Stalin's war on capitalism meant the extermination of the "bourgeois mentality" and the creation of an entirely new society. All the social institutions of the past came under attack, and centralized control of every aspect of soviet life accompanied centralization of the economy. Family life weakened as the soviet agencies actively worked to undermine parental and traditional authority. Strict censorship insured that the newspapers, literature, movies, the theatre, art and music applauded and proclaimed the Soviet ideology. In the schools teachers were closely supervised and textbooks were written to indoctrinate young Communist minds.

Since religion was considered a stronghold of traditional thought, the Soviet leadership sharply curtailed religious activity. Church property was confiscated and churches converted into museums or other types of secular buildings. Religious publications were forbidden, civil marriages encouraged, and religious instruction outlawed.

After Hitler's advent to power in 1933, however, and the increase of Japanese aggression in the Far East, the Soviet leadership realized that it needed widespread support for the regime in case of war. The announced success of the First Five Year Plan permitted a slight relaxation of the ruthless drive toward industrialization. Government social policies eased, and propaganda began to insist on the importance of healthy family discipline and the recognition of parental authority. Even the attack on religion was reversed to the extent that at one time the Party-sponsored Atheist Society was ordered to rehabilitate the church. Perhaps most significantly, emphasis changed from the international revolutionary nature of the Communist movement to old-fashioned Russian nationalism. Old heroes, even those from Tsarist times, were dusted off and refurbished, and used as examples of good communists. All this meant that Russia was moving farther and farther away from the kind of international proletarian society Karl Marx had envisioned and was developing a new system marked more by Russia's national heritage than by socialist philosophy. The Russian Soviet State, as it emerged, blended a harsh political dictatorship with a socialist economy, but the chances that the state would ever "wither away" as Marx had predicted diminished yearly.

• The Constitution of 1936 and Stalin's Totalitarianism

The Constitution of 1936 contributed to building support for the Soviet regime. It served well the propaganda interests of the communists abroad, as well, for it seemed remarkably democratic to outsiders, and it seemed to signify the end of the harsh struggle to establish the society. Although guarantees of the basic freedoms considered essential in the West were absent, fewer Russians than we might imagine were distressed by the omission. The Constitution appeared to provide for the participation of the individual citizen in the political system. It did guarantee "universal, direct and equal suffrage by secret ballot" and decreed that all citizens of eighteen years or older, "irrespective of race, nationality, religion, educational and residential qualifications, social origin, property status or past activities, have the right to vote . . . and to be elected. . . ." In practice, during the first elections, each electoral district presented several candidates. The Party selected one for each position, the ballot showed only one name, and the voter could vote yes or no. Ninety-six percent of the eligible voters cast ballots; of those, 98 percent voted yes. The existence of only one party obviously precluded the possibility of the democratic process, but to the vast majority of Russians the system was infinitely superior to anything else they had known.

In reality the new Constitution marked very little change in the rule of force which characterized Stalin's regime. At the very time that the document was being praised by westerners, Stalin set out to eliminate the Old Bolsheviks, who retained ideas antithetic to Stalinist communism. In a series of purges which lasted from 1934 to 1938, Stalin reached into every segment of the governmental structure to eradicate deviation and brought even high officials to trial. Western observers were astonished at the eagerness with which most of the accused pleaded guilty to the charges, and with the rapidity with which they were convicted and sentenced. Nearly all were executed. Through the purges Stalin destroyed all opposition to his personal rule, and removed all the old idealists who had dreamed of establishing a truly democratic system of socialism, with the state withering away, and with even high government officials receiving no more privileges than laborers. Perhaps Stalin genuinely feared conspiracies from both right and left opposition forces to his dictatorship – and certainly he later developed a distrust of everyone which bordered on madness. Before the purges ended, Stalin bore the responsibility for the deaths of three-quarters of a million party members.

After the purges new young men trained and brainwashed in the Stalinist era refilled the ranks of the party. By 1939 Stalin's totalitarian control was unchallenged, with the dictator revered almost as a god. Any new opposition would have to be secret and desperate, and would risk torture and death. The purges ended finally and completely any possibility of change by discussion, compromise, or yielding on the part of government. Henceforth Stalinist totalitarianism became increasingly rigid and inflexible, and Russia a closed society. Each new step in the direction of Stalinist communism further alienated the West — and added fuel to the fires the Fascists built to weaken opposition to their expansionist exploits.

• Clash of Ideologies: Aggression and Appeasement

The "Era of Locarno," that period of apparent peace and reconciliation between the European powers in the years after 1925, did not last long. It was, in reality, a period of false security — the calm before the storm. England and France, undisputed leaders in the diplomatic maneuverings of the European nations after 1919, could not develop a cooperative policy. Because their underlying convictions about Germany were fundamentally irreconcilable, they frequently pulled in opposing directions rather than exerting firm leadership together. They did, however, agree completely about one thing — the necessity of isolating Russia from European affairs. At the same time the United States withdrew deeper and deeper into isolationism and abdicated responsibility in European concerns. The failure of these four powers to consolidate their combined strength and forcefully oppose violations of the peace made World War II a certainty from the time of the first Fascist challenges of the peace.

The weakness of British and French foreign policy was not immediately obvious. The League of Nations had been created to provide collective security against aggression. The smaller nations in particular had high hopes that it would do so. But the League got little support from the Great Powers. Neither the United States nor Russia was a member, and England supported it only when it suited her to do so. By the early 1930's France's domestic problems had so absorbed the attention and energies of her statesmen that she felt incapable of strong action without British support, and Britain refused to take a strong stand against Fascist expansion.

During the years after World War I the western democracies, struggling with internal economic and political dislocations, developed a policy of conciliation in the face of aggression which the Fascist dictators understood only as weakness. The policy of granting concessions to a dictator's demands when threatened with force became known as the appeasement policy. Appeasing the dictators generated from a genuine fear of another war, a fear complicated by the conviction, in the leadership of both England and France, that a new war would open the floodgates to Bolshevik revolution all over Europe. In England, the unquestionable leader in the genesis and evolution of the appeasement policy, a sincere conviction that Germany had been badly treated by the Versailles peace settlement contributed to the belief that a restitution of Germany's honorable position would satisfy her ambitions and eventually result in stability in Central Europe. The English belief that Hitler represented "the last bulwark against Communism" further reinforced the policy. All of these factors combined to paralyze British diplomacy, and the British refusal to act paralyzed the French. In short, American and Russian isolation, the weakness of the League and the British and French abdication of strong leadership convinced the Fascist aggressors that no real opposition to their ambitions existed. They gradually moved more and more openly down a path of aggression that finally led to war.

• Early Aggression

The inability of the League of Nations to deal effectively with outright aggression was clearly demonstrated in 1931 when the Japanese seized Manchuria. China appealed to the League for help. The League took months to adopt a report which mildly criticized the Japanese for their tactics but suggested that the Chinese concede to Japanese demands. Individual states such as England chose to refuse to sell arms to either side, a policy which assisted the industrialized Japanese whose resources required no outside assistance against economically backward China. The League's failure to resist the Japanese military threat caused a general loss of respect for the organization, as both great and small powers recognized its ineffectual nature.

After the Nazis attained power in Germany, aggression accelerated. In 1935 Adolf Hitler announced to the world that Germany would reintroduce conscription and universal military training. Such a direct violation of the Versailles Treaty would have merited instant reprisal from England and France had it been announced by the Weimar government, but the German democrats no longer represented Germany. An expansive, militant leadership, ruthless and totalitarian, now spoke for Germany to a world wracked by the Great Depression, serious domestic problems, and often a number of Fascist sympathizers. France wished to oppose the German decree but feared to take action alone. England responded by signing a treaty with Germany which allowed Germany to begin rebuilding her navy.

Hitler's next step was an even more serious violation of the Treaty of Versailles. Perhaps more significantly, it violated the Treaty of Locarno, which by no stretch of the imagination had been forced on the Germans. In March, 1936 German troops reoccupied the Rhineland, the area bordering France which had been demilitarized after World War I. Hitler could have been easily stopped at that time with any, even the slightest, show of force. His personal orders to his generals instructed them to retreat if they met any resistance at all. But, again, France found no support either in England or the United States, and she had no heart to move alone. Soon hundreds of thousands of German workers began fortifying the area which would protect Germany from possible attack while she pursued her adventures in the East and South.

• Italy's Ethiopian Venture

Germany was not the only country in Europe practicing aggression. Italy, like Germany a latecomer to the community of nations, felt that she, too, should have colonies. Particularly she believed that Ethiopia should belong to Italy, and had attempted in the late nineteenth century to conquer it. The Ethiopians at that time had proved too much for the Italian military, however, and the defeat had increased the frustration of those Italian nationalists who clamored for Italian territorial additions. Now Benito Mussolini made the decision to incorporate the Ethiopians into the Italian empire. In 1935 the Italians organized border incidents to provide an excuse for an invasion. The Ethiopian government, a member of the League of Nations since 1923, naturally appealed to the League; the League received the appeal but failed to act. In March, 1935 Ethiopia again appealed to the League with evidence that Italy planned immediate invasion. This time the League was busy with the fears which Germany's announced military draft had generated and again chose not to act. Only after the Italians had launched a full-scale invasion into Ethiopia did the League do anything at all and then its action approached the farcical. Economic sanctions were applied against Italy — that is, member nations of the League agreed not to sell the Italians munitions or materials which would aid their military efforts. The sanctions, however, carefully excluded oil, the one commodity most needed by the Italian war machine. Italy could also have been stopped cold simply by closing the Suez Canal to her military use, but that was not done. The Ethiopian capital fell in May, 1935 — shortly thereafter the entire country was incorporated into Italy's empire. Once again the aggressive power had achieved its goal while the democratic powers practiced appeasement, hoping that the dictators' desires would be satiated before they attacked the larger states.

• The Spanish Civil War

The year 1936 dealt another body blow to the League of Nations and to the hopes for peace and reasonable solutions to world problems. During that year the aggressor states formed an alliance which stretched across the world from Germany to Japan. In October, Hitler and Mussolini signed a formal agreement known as the Rome-Berlin Axis, which they intended to be the basis for determining European diplomacy. In the following month Germany and Japan signed a pact which had as its public clauses opposition to the world-wide communist movement, but which included secret clauses providing for military cooperation against Russia as a state. The imperialistic powers had joined together in the Rome-Berlin-Tokyo Axis – the nucleus for World War II.

Almost immediately, the new Fascist bonds were strengthened by joint participation in the Spanish Civil War. Spain had made little progress toward modernization until 1931. Most of her population were poor, illiterate peasants, miserably exploited by an arrogant nobility, a few wealthy capitalists, the remarkably corrupt officers of the army, and the determinedly medieval Roman Catholic Church. In 1931 a bloodless revolution established a new Republic, with a liberal democratic constitution. The new government immediately launched an effort to modernize Spain. Church and State were separated, the Jesuit order dissolved, and civil marriage permitted in an effort to break the Church's strangle-hold on the population.

Every new piece of social legislation and reform, however, angered the former ruling classes and made them more intransigent. The Land Reform Bill of 1932, an effort to redistribute the land, caused the entire right wing to coalesce into opposition to the government. Monarchists, landlords, and army officers joined with the most determined opponents of all, the Catholic Church, in opposition to the Republic. Bishops forbade Spanish children to attend the state schools, and Pope Pius XI issued an encyclical condemning the Republic and all its acts. The result was that in the general election of 1933, with the Pope actively participating in the electioneering, the right wing elements gained a majority in the government and promptly set about to turn the clock back. As they hastily undid everything the republican government had accomplished, the left wing opposition began to solidify. In 1936 the left formed a Popular Front and won a clear majority in the 1936 elections.

Rather than lose their positions of power and wealth, the Conservatives chose to overthrow the republic and restore the old regime by force. Under the leadership of General Francisco Franco, and with the active participation of the Spanish Fascist Party (the Falange), the right wing opened armed rebellion against the constitutional government, beginning the Spanish Civil War.

Hitler and Mussolini quickly recognized the opportunity to gain prestige for Fascism by adding another Fascist dictatorship to the growing

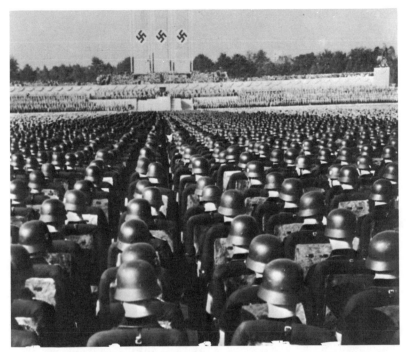

120,000 Nazi Storm Troopers under Review by Hitler at Nuremberg in 1938. World Wide Photos.

list. General Franco appealed for and at once received military support from both Germany and Italy. Germany sent the cream of her military to prepare them to serve later as training cadres for her own armies, rotating them, experimenting with new equipment, using Spain as a testing ground for her future military endeavors. Italy ultimately sent six army corps, fully equipped with planes, tanks, and artillery. In the decisive battles of the Spanish Civil War more Italians fought in Franco's army than did Spaniards.

The Loyalists appealed to the democracies for help, but they once more chose appeasement. England, France, and the United States insisted on strict neutrality, a hands-off policy which prevented any but a few Russian troops and scattered volunteer units from helping the Loyalists. By 1939, after incredible slaughter and vicious brutality, the Loyalists were destroyed and Franco established a dictatorship which survived to his death. Facism benefitted enormously from the episode, but the morale and influence of the democratic countries suffered. The Spanish Civil War marks a turning point on the road to World War II.

• Germany Annexes Austria

Each successive step in the aggression-appeasement pattern strengthened the dictators and encouraged further challenges to the peace while it made the appeasers more timorous. By 1937 Hitler was convinced that he could annex Austria and Czechoslovakia without provoking a general war. He saw England as the crucial opponent, and England had convinced him that she would not take action so long as Hitler's objectives lay in the center and eastern portions of Europe. Actually, England's leaders hoped that Germany and Russia, declared enemies, would go to war against each other. The Austrian Nazis belligerently insisted that all Austrians wanted their country to join the Third Reich. Hitler provided them with moral support by making public speeches in which he proclaimed himself the protector of the millions of Germans living outside the Fatherland. In 1938 he demanded that the Austrian Chancellor, Kurt von Schuschnigg, appoint one of his henchmen to the cabinet. Schuschnigg feared to refuse, but feared also the consequences of giving in. As the Austrian Nazis went on a rampage, Schuschnigg in desperation decided on a plebiscite to determine whether the majority of Austrians really wanted to join the Third Reich and called an election for March 9. Afraid he would lose the vote, Hitler moved troops into invasion position on the Austrian border and announced that unless Schuschnigg called off the plebiscite, he would order invasion. Schuschnigg resigned and a Nazi became Chancellor and immediately invited the German army into Austria. France and England once again acquiesced rather than fight. Before the month was out, Hitler had ordered his military advisers to prepare the invasion plans for Czechoslovakia.

• Annexation of Czechoslovakia

Czechoslovakia, carved out of the old Hapsburg Empire after 1918, was made up of a number of drastically different peoples and economies. The highly industrialized Czechs tended to dominate the other nationalities and to insist on a highly centralized state with a large degree of socialism in the economy. The Slovaks, heavily rural and Catholic, wanted states' rights within the system. Even more serious were the differences between the Czechs and the Sudeten Germans. Some three and a half million Germans, occupying the Sudetenland, an area bordering Germany, had lost their special position in the Austrian Empire with its dissolution. Using the argument of self-determination, they demanded special privileges

Europe - 1941
Before German Invasion of Russia

of the Czech government. By 1935, under the leadership of Konrad Henlein, the Sudeten Germans had formed a Nazi Party which looked to Hitler as its real leader, and which became the largest political party in the area.

Hitler's propaganda machine kept up a barrage of lies about terrible Czech mistreatment of the Sudeten Germans, insisting that the Czech government was a tool of Russia. Under such pressure, the government granted concessions to the Sudetens, but by 1938 Henlein refused to accept anything less than unification of the Sudeten area with Germany. After the Austrian *Anschluss* Hitler publicly stated that he would use force if necessary to bring about annexation of the Sudetenland.

Czechoslovakia prepared for war, and called on her allies, France, Russia, Rumania, and Yugoslavia, to fulfill their agreements to support her should Germany attack. But appeasement decreed otherwise. France delayed, looking to England for support, and England refused to fight to preserve the independence and integrity of Czechoslovakia. Instead of pledging resistance to the German demands, Neville Chamberlain, the British Prime Minister, sent a representative to Czechoslovakia to urge the Czechs to permit the country's dismemberment. Russia's firm offer of support caused the Czechs and the western nations more distress than did the possibility of another German victory. A frantic series of meetings resulted in a final conference at Munich in late September, 1938. Neither the Russians nor the Czechs were invited to attend the Munich Conference, the meeting at which the Germans were given one fourth of Czechoslovakia's land area, one third of her population, including many non-Germans, and all of her defenses.

Neville Chamberlain has received most of the opprobrium for this best-known example of appeasement and certainly he deserves some. But the Munich Cession was hailed at the time all over Europe and in the United States as the most suitable solution to a dangerous threat to world peace. Few could see that a peace bought with such dishonor would be shortlived, and that even the time bought worked in Germany's favor, as she was arming at a faster rate than the western democracies. Furthermore, Czechoslovakia had been a democratic stronghold, with a powerful, well-equipped army and rich industrial resources. Now that army, and the resources, went to the side of the Fascists. At the same time Russia, deliberately excluded from European decisions, properly decided that she would have to look after herself. A straight line runs from Russia's exclusion from the Munich Conference to the Nazi-Soviet Non-Aggression Pact of August 23, 1939.

• The Last Step

Although the western powers did nothing to oppose Hitler's annexation of the rest of Czechoslovakia in the spring of 1939, it was nevertheless now clear, even to Chamberlain, that Hitler must be stopped. Everyone knew that Poland was Hitler's next target. Awkward as it might seem at this late date, England, France, and Poland now signed a pact in which all agreed that an attack on one would be looked upon as an attack on all, and all would fight to prevent further aggression. England and France thereby guaranteed the independence of Poland. The British and French even attempted to negotiate with Russia, but the courtship was half-hearted and Russia's price had gone up after Munich — she demanded annexations to which England and France could not agree. Germany offered Russia the territory she demanded, and the two nations, once bitter enemies, quickly came to agreement. The Nazi-Soviet Pact of August,

1939, concluded in a matter of weeks, agreed that Russia could annex part of Poland and all of the Baltic states, Latvia, Estonia, and Lithuania.

Once Hitler was assured of Russian acquiescence to his further expansion, he no longer feared the opposition of France and England. Convinced, despite their guarantee to the contrary, that the western nations were effete and would not actually fight, he openly prepared for an invasion of Poland. One week after the Nazi-Soviet Pact was announced to a surprised world, the Germans advanced. On September 1, 1939, after twenty years of an unstable and constantly threatened peace, World War II began.

● **World War II: The Old World Dies**

German military leaders had learned well the lessons of World War I. Then, because the war had turned into a war of attrition and had lasted far beyond their short-range preparation, they had been beaten by superior economic and manpower resources. Now the Germans concentrated on developing a military machine which was specifically designed to prevent stalemate and trench warfare. World War I had been almost wholly defensive in its strategy. The Germans planned World War II as pure offense. Instead of using tanks merely as a protective wall (a mobile trench), the generals organized entire divisions of tanks designed to break directly through the defense of the enemy and to operate without immediate reference to infantry at all. The air force, limited in World War I to spotting for artillery, romantic dog-fighting, and tossing bombs out by hand, now was prepared to wreak major destruction by mass bombing and to support the infantry by strafing and bombing immediately ahead of its advance. The totality of offense came to be known as Blitzkrieg (Lightning War).

● **Blitzkrieg and Sitzkrieg**

A few individuals in the West had the same ideas, and the French built some excellent tanks, the British fine planes. But the mentality remained the mentality of World War I. The French, obsessed with defensive strategy, built the Maginot Line, massive fortifications from Switzerland to Belgium, and planned to wait for the Germans to wear themselves out against this impregnable fortress.

The Germans did not oblige. Leaving only token forces in the West, they struck Poland with almost the entire German army. Poland's air force never got off the ground and was wiped out on September 1, 1939. The tank divisions ripped through the Polish defenses with ease. By mid-September only Warsaw, completely surrounded, held out. Retreating Poles ran into the Russians, who had hastily advanced to be sure they got the territory they had been promised in the Nazi-Soviet Pact. Before the month was out Russia and Germany had divided Poland, wiping it off the map. Russia took a little more than half the territory and a little less than half the population. Germany got the rest.

Russia turned immediately to the establishment of military control over Latvia, Lithuania, and Estonia, with a series of treaties in September and October, 1939. Efforts to gain control over Finland and Turkey proved more troublesome. Turkey relied upon her alliances with the West and rejected the Russian demands, whereupon Russia let the matter ride. Finland chose war rather than to yield, and for a few months startled the world by her magnificent and futile efforts against Russia in the "Winter War." By March, 1940, however, the victorious Russians had forced even harsher terms than originally demanded from the Finns, and had left Finland largely defenseless.

During all this time the western states, theoretically in a state of war with Germany, had done nothing. Stunned by the awesome effects of the *Blitzkrieg* in Poland, western military leaders convinced themselves even more strongly that defense was the only possible weapon and so kept their increasingly unhappy soldiers hidden behind the Maginot Line. The winter of 1939-1940 came to be known as the *Sitzkrieg* — sitting war — or the Phony War.

• The Fall of France

The Germans were simply biding their time, however. The lightning struck again in April, 1940 — this time on Denmark and Norway. Denmark fell at once and although Norway resisted she could not last long under the new methods of warfare. Paratroops seized control of airfields which immediately received Nazi troops, transports, and equipment. The Germans were assisted by the treason of some Norwegians, most notably Vidkun Quisling, who were repaid by being permitted to establish a satellite regime after the conquest. After the attack on Norway, the word "quisling" entered the English language as a synonym for treason and fifth-column activity.

Having completely sealed his back doors, Hitler was ready to take on his major enemies and to invade the West. On May 10, 1940 he advanced into Belgium, Holland, and Luxemburg. Luxemburg chose not to fight, Holland lasted five days, and the Belgians surrendered on May 28. But the Germans had not waited for that event — they were sitting on the English Channel on May 20, already in French territory.

The speed of the German movement owed much to the rigid defense thinking of the Allies, particularly the French. The Maginot Line had magnificent defenses, but most Frenchmen had never bothered to worry that it extended only from Switzerland to the Belgian border. The Germans simply launched their attack around the end of the Maginot Line, where France, Germany, and Belgium met. The Belgian surrender, without prior warning to the Allies, left the British and French Expeditionary Forces exposed to a vastly superior German army, without support from the main French army. They were forced back to the Channel and stranded at Dunkirk. The English utilized every kind of floating vessel at their disposal and evacuated 230,000 British and French soldiers in a heroic rescue operation. But they left another half million behind, captured or killed. And all of their equipment, artillery, and supplies fell into German hands.

Meanwhile, ignoring the Maginot defenses, the Germans pushed rapidly on to Paris, occupying the city on June 13. The French, bewildered and demoralized by the failure of their defenses, hastened to make peace with Germany. A new government agreed to German occupation of more than half of France, including all her coasts, with the French people paying the occupation costs. The government of unoccupied France, established with the capital at Vichy, soon became nothing more than a dictatorial puppet of Adolf Hitler. A few French chose to fight on, and gradually grouped around an indomitable fighter, General Charles DeGaulle. Operating from London, DeGaulle's troops became the Free French forces who fought on with the English for the liberation of all France. Germany's rapid conquest of France, however, finally brought Hitler's ally, Mussolini, into the war.

After the fall of France England stood alone facing a Europe almost entirely occupied by Hitler's troops or his allies. Hitler's plans for the invasion of England depended on German control of the air and sea around the island. For months the German air force attempted to establish air superiority, bombing British industrial cities and towns daily and wreaking awesome damage. But the British, courageously rallying to defend their independence, shot down three German planes for every English plane lost. Hitler could never gain sufficient control to permit an invasion and lost the Battle of Britain. The Germans were running out of fuel, and abandoned the operations against England.

- **The Russian Invasion**

Hitler had never intended to abide permanently by his non-aggression pact with Russia — Communism had always been his most bitterly denounced foe. He had begun planning an invasion of the Soviet Union immediately after the conquest of France. In June, 1941 he put his plans into action, and turned to the invasion of Russia. In a very real sense, it marked a turning point in the war. As bitterly as Russia had been isolated and opposed by everyone in the western world in the years before the war, Hitler's attack enlisted the sympathy of the free world for Russia. In a surprising turn-about, the long antagonism between communism and democracy was forgotten, and Americans, British, and Free French began to hope that Russia would defeat Germany.

At first the *Blitzkrieg* appeared to have the same success in the Russian invasion that it had previously enjoyed in the West. By December, 1941 the Germans held an area of Russia equal to nearly 20 percent of the size of the entire United States. But the Russians had yielded ground without losing control; they had practiced a "scorched earth" policy, removing or destroying everything of use in the path of the Germans, and their armies remained intact. As winter weather slowed the German advance, the Russian defense tightened. In December the Russians launched a counter-attack all along a line from Leningrad to Moscow to the eastern tip of the Sea of Azov, forcing the Germans back until Hitler ordered his men not to retreat, even if it meant certain death. But the Germans were not prepared for a Russian winter, since Hitler had expected complete victory before the winter months, so they suffered heavily. After the spring thaw the Germans returned to the offensive and drove this time all the way to Stalingrad, where Stalin ordered the Russians to hold. Hold they did, in an awesome house-to-house battle which killed nearly 300,000 Axis soldiers and broke the German offensive. After the Battle of Stalingrad the Russians went on the offensive and did not stop until they were masters of Berlin.

- **The United States Enters the War**

In the United States, although the sympathies of the people clearly lay with England and France during the early phases of the war, isolationism had been responsible for legislation which forbade any action that might involve the United States in war. As the peace steadily deteriorated during the 1930's, Congress passed neutrality legislation aimed at keeping

America entirely out of the threatening European conflict. In 1935 a law prevented the sale of any goods to any country involved in war, and in 1937 further legislation made it clear that victims of aggression could expect no more help from the United States than could the aggressors. Exports could be made only on a cash-and-carry basis, and Americans, deluding themselves about Hitler's plans for world domination, believed that whatever happened in Europe was of no concern to them. American oil shipments gave tremendous support to Mussolini in his Ethiopian venture. During the Spanish Civil War American policy (specified by law in 1937) prevented the sale of arms even to the legal and constitutional government of Spain, although at the same time war materials were sold to Japan which aided in the conquests in China. Refugees with no place to go found no haven in the United States since the quota system limiting immigration permitted entry to very few Europeans.

After the fall of France, however, Americans recognized reluctantly that they could not remain totally uninvolved. As it became increasingly obvious that England could not indefinitely stand alone, Congress permitted the "destroyers-for-bases" deal, which traded half a hundred worn-out destroyers to England in return for U.S. control over English territory to be used for military bases. Finally, in March, 1941, in a sudden decision to make the United States "the arsenal of democracy," Congress authorized the President to lend or lease support to England, when it became evident that that country had food supplies for only a short time and would soon fall before the Nazi onslaught. After the invasion of Russia, Americans woke up to Hitler's goals of European domination. Congress repealed the neutrality laws, and the United States began a far more active participation in the effort to stop Hitler, sending money and supplies to both England and Russia.

Events in the Far East, however, finally brought America directly into the war. On December 7, 1941 the Japanese struck against the United States in the Pacific. Using aircraft carriers to bring their bombers and fighter planes to Pearl Harbor, they attacked and destroyed the better part of America's Pacific fleet and much of her air power. On the same day another attack did massive damage to American forces in the Philippines. The United States declared war on Japan the following day. Japan's allies, Germany and Italy, then declared war on the United States. Consequently, the Americans, drawn unwillingly into the European inferno, determined to cooperate with England and Russia in beating the Germans first, while operating a holding action against the other Axis powers.

American entry made a tremendous difference in the European theater of war. Turning her awesome industrial capacity into the war effort, she supplied her allies with vast quantities of armaments while she built her own army and navy into formidable forces. Before the war ended Americans built nearly 300,000 airplanes, some 3,000,000 machine guns, 85,000 tanks, 8,000,000 tons of ships for the Navy, and 55,000,000 tons of merchant ships.

In 1942 Americans joined the British in North Africa, until that time a dangerously weak area for the British army. With American support in new landings, the German and Italian forces in Africa were caught between American and British armies and forced to surrender. The Allies were still not ready, however, for a direct assault on the continent, and chose instead to move into Sicily. But that operation brought German troops far south into Italy, and an American force was landed on the peninsula below Naples. The British joined in the drive and gradually, at tremendous cost, the Allies pushed north. The Germans, however, were never cleared out of northern Italy until the end of the war.

In the meantime the great buildup for the direct invasion across the English Channel had been proceeding. On June 6, 1944, after heavy air and naval bombardment and simultaneous paratroop landings, the first wave of Allied soldiers hit the Normandy beaches, and soon secured a beach-head sufficiently strong to pack in the main invasion army and its equipment. A second landing took place from the Mediterranean, and soon more than two and a half million Allied soldiers were pushing the Germans out of France and looking toward an invasion of Germany itself. A desperate German counter-attack failed, and in the spring of 1945 the Russians and western Allies met in Germany. At about the same time Mussolini was captured and shot by Italian partisans. Hitler chose suicide rather than capture by the Russians as they destroyed Berlin. The Germans, without their demonic leader to push them to further destruction, surrendered on May 7, 1945.

• War in the Far East

In the Far East the United States remained on the defensive for the most part throughout 1942, although in two major sea-battles, Coral Sea and Midway, the American navy seriously damaged the Japanese navy. In 1943 the buildup was sufficient for American forces to take the offensive and recapture many of the islands which had fallen to the Japanese the previous year. The battles of the Philippine Sea and Leyte Gulf in June and October, 1944 broke the back of the Japanese navy and permitted American forces to retake the Philippines. By the spring of 1945 American planes were dropping bombs on Japanese cities, while plans were laid for the invasion of Japan. In the meantime, however, American scientists had perfected an awesome new weapon. In August, 1945 American planes dropped atomic bombs on Hiroshima and Nagasaki, literally destroying the cities and killing some 200,000 people. The Japanese surrendered on August 14, 1945, and the war was over.

• Assessment

But the full horrors of the war still had to be assimilated. The Second World War, more than the first, had indeed been global war, wreaking devastation, horror, and death that is difficult to comprehend even when the full evidence is presented. World War I challenged the Enlightenment beliefs in rationalism and progress which the nineteenth century had accepted with almost religious intensity, but did not destroy them. After World War II, the European world realized that the nineteenth-century certainties had been proven indisputably false. As the Allied armies advanced through German territory, the grisly obscenities of the Nazi regime were revealed to a world already stunned by the atrocities of war. The liberation of the concentration camps exposed in ghastly detail the extent of Fascist insanity. Some six million Jews from conquered German territories had been tortured and killed in Auschwitz, Bergen-Belsen, Buchenwald, Dachau, and similar camps. In Auschwitz alone in 1944 as many as 22,000 Jews were processed, gassed, and cremated every day. German industry and agriculture utilized slave labor, collected clothing and shoes of victims, used their bones for fertilizer. The bankers received gold fillings from the victims' teeth, while scientists practised gruesome experiments on their bodies. The barbaric cruelties in the camps provided horrifying evidence of the total breakdown of civilization in the twentieth century. World War II proved, even to those most reluctant to admit it, that twentieth-century man was not rational — that the forces of hatred, aggression, and cruelty had overwhelmed rationality and destroyed progress. No longer could man cling to the old solutions — the twentieth-century experiments had exposed the bankruptcy of most of the old verities. World War II left the world without illusions. In the post-war world, new hopes had somehow to be found.

Suggestions for Further Reading

Two general works spanning the first half of the twentieth century are Raymond James Sontag, *A Broken World: 1919-1939* (1971) and John Terraine, *The Mighty Continent* (1975), and Alastair Horne, *The Price of Glory: Verdun, 1916* (1963). Jack Roth, ed., *World War I: A Turning Point in Modern History* (1967) shows how the war shaped the course of post-war European development. Norman Stone, *The Eastern Front, 1914-1917* (1976) offers new explanations for Russia's failure in the war. Harold Nicholson, *Peacemaking 1919* (1939) is a classic description of the Versailles Conference by a participant.

Useful studies of the evolution of Russian Communist society are J.P. Nettl, *The Soviet Achievement* (1968), William L. Blackwell, *The Industrialization of Russia* (1970), and Alec Nove, *Stalinism and After* (1975). Antony Polansky, *The Little Dictators: The History of Eastern Europe since 1918* (1975) is good for eastern Europe. Good overviews of fascism are Eugen Weber, *Varieties of Fascism* (1964) and Francis L. Carstens, *The Rise of Fascism* (1967). On the Weimer Republic consult William S. Halperin, *Germany Tried Democracy* (1946); Alan Cassels, *Fascist Italy* (1968), is brief and comprehensive. The best biography of Mussolini to date is Ivone Kirkpatrick, *Mussolini: A Study of Power* (1964).

Among the highly readable accounts of the background of World War II are Joachim Remak, *The Origins of the Second World War* (1976), Roger Parkinson, *Peace for our Time* (1972), and Sidney Aster, *1939: The Making of the Second World War* (1974). Gordon Wright, *The Ordeal of Total War, 1939-1945* (1968) discusses the war itself, as does Martha Byrd Hoyle, *A World in Flames: A History of World War II* (1970). Terry Hughes and John Costello, *The Battle of the Atlantic* (1977) is a gripping account of the war at sea. Anthony Cave Brown, *Bodyguard of Lies* (1976) discusses Allied intelligence and preparation for the D-day invasion.

GENESIS OF A NEW WORLD
1945 TO THE PRESENT

21

The Era of Cold War

WHEN THE GUNS stopped in 1945, the world rejoiced that the grueling years of the Second World War had ended. But the delirium was short-lived. The war left a legacy of almost total devastation in Europe and loosed a tidal wave of political and social unrest that swept every nation in the world. A new age began in 1945, although few realized it at the time.

The war's most obvious legacy was enormous material and social destruction. Reconstruction was the most pressing and most immediate task. Almost the entire European continent had to be rebuilt politically, agriculturally, and industrially. Many of Europe's major cities — Berlin, Warsaw, Dresden, Stalingrad — were in ashes; others, like London and Vienna, had suffered extensive and crippling damage. Many smaller cities in Germany, France, and Russia had been razed to the ground. In the battle zones little of anything remained — communication and transportation systems were ruined, industry destroyed. Restoration of agriculture presented staggering problems, as many areas were not in condition for cultivation, and livestock and machinery were unavailable.

• The Effects of War

The cost of the war had drained the monetary resources of the belligerent nations. Although estimates are not exact, war costs have been calculated at more than $1,000 billion. The United States and Germany contributed the greatest sums — Americans spent $317 billion, the Germans $273 billion — but every nation had squeezed its economy to the last penny to support the war effort. Damage to civilian property added several billion dollars to the total sums.

These figures indicate the economic exhaustion which the war caused in every nation in Europe. But human resources were as depleted by the war as were material resources; Europe's population declined by 30 million. Hitler's attempt to eliminate the entire Jewish race took six million lives. Admittedly uncertain statistics calculated military deaths at more than 15 million — Germany lost 3,500,000, while 7,500,000 Russians were killed. But concentration camp victims and military casualties only partially account for the victims of World War II. Civilian populations were more directly involved in this war than in any war in history, and it is impossible to calculate the lives lost in the air-raids and bombing of cities or through the starvation and disease which inevitably accompanied the war. The psychological effect of death in such staggering numbers is impossible to describe. Scarcely a single family in all of Europe emerged unscathed — in simple terms, this means that every individual member of the European population suffered the emotional after-effects of the war. The Nazi reign of terror left scars which many have not yet overcome.

Death accounted only partially for the decimation of European national populations — additional millions had been displaced from their homes. Prisoners, expatriated minorities, fugitives, refugees from every country crowded the roads of Europe. In the years immediately following the war, possibly 30 million people had to be relocated, or returned to their homes. The reintegration of these war victims posed formidable problems in housing, jobs, and social organization for governments already over-burdened with reconstruction problems.

And reconstruction included necessary political rebuilding. Many formerly strong nations — France, Italy, and Germany among others — were politically broken as well. The Fascist regimes and their puppet administrations had been destroyed and new governments had to be constructed to replace them. The border countries in East Europe struggled to reestablish political systems — most attempted for the second time since 1919 to broaden the base of political participation and to build democratic regimes. Even the British, so strongly united during the war, encountered forceful demands for change both at home and in the Empire. In the post-war decade economic reconstruction and political reorganization absorbed most of the energies of European statesmen.

- ## The Superpowers

Europe's exhaustion left a vacuum of power in world politics; the war destroyed the balance of power which formerly ruled international affairs. England, Russia, and the United States had controlled the Grand Coalition which dominated the war effort. But England's participation depleted her strength, and after the war her influence rapidly declined. In the two decades after the war the formerly great British Empire sank to the status of a minor world power along with the other European states. Only two nations sustained enough vitality to continue to exert leadership – Russia and the United States.

The United States was unquestionably the most fortunate of the belligerent nations to emerge from the war. Industrial production rose to new heights, and the demands of the American people for consumer goods curbed even the fear of post-war inflation. The war effort restored confidence in American institutions and produced a conviction that the country could and should play a large role in the post-war world. There were minor problems: demobilization had to be accomplished and the released veterans absorbed into the economy; inflation did exist; and a flurry of strikes indicated that the labor force intended to participate in the benefits of the new affluence. But on the whole Americans faced the peace confident, strong, and optimistic.

Russia, too, managed to avoid the psychologically defeated attitude which characterized the other European states. Although she suffered massive property damage in Western Russia and lost more dead than any country (15 to 21 million dead), her leaders and people convinced themselves that danger to her social experiment still existed, and she retained a strongly militant stand. She therefore continued to pursue an aggressive policy, determined to recover all the territorial losses she had suffered after World War I, and to establish a sphere of influence in Eastern Europe which would serve as an effective defensive perimeter between the Soviet Union and the West. Nor had Stalin completely abandoned the ultimate goal of world communist revolution. In pursuit of that aim he actively encouraged leftist revolts whenever the opportunity arose. Moreover, Russia's industrial machinery had been built only in the immediate pre-war decade. It was new, modern, and much of it had survived the war. Russia's productive capacity consequently remained strong at war's end, capable of supporting both Russian reconstruction and Russian imperialistic ambitions.

Japan's defeat in the Far East and China's continued weakness meant that Russian and American supremacy could not be challenged in the Pacific; Europe's exhaustion assured that no challenge would arise in the West. There arose, then, a new phenomenon — two superpowers, whose influence determined the course of world affairs. Bipolarity of power would be one of the distinguishing characteristics of the new era until cooperation between the smaller nations of the world began, in the 1960s, to indicate a new dissemination of power. When Russia acquired the atomic bomb in 1949, the Russian and American ascendancy was finalized — the two atomic powers indisputably held greater military strength than the rest of the world combined.

• The United Nations

Even before the final failure of the old international balance and the emergence of bipolarity the realization of the interdependence of twentieth-century nations, so clearly demonstrated by the Second World War, provoked a search for new forms of international organization. Although the League of Nations had singularly failed to preserve peace in the inter-war period, the concept of a multi-national arena in which sovereign states could work in harmony to promote the welfare of mankind survived, and created the United Nations.

In 1941 Roosevelt and Churchill issued the Atlantic Charter, an idealistic statement of war aims which recognized the importance of international cooperation in developing economic prosperity and preserving peace, and suggested "the establishment of a wider and permanent system of general security." The following year 26 states signed a "Declaration of United Nations," pledging united action against the Axis Powers. These states were to become the charter members of the formal body of the United Nations when it organized in 1945.

The formal proposal for "a general international organization" came from a Moscow conference of the United States, Russia, England, and China in 1943, and the following year the United States hosted a meeting to draft plans for the organization. When the leaders of the Allied Coalition — Roosevelt, Churchill, and Stalin — met to confer at Yalta in February, 1945, they acted on the proposals and scheduled an interna-

Prime Minister Winston Churchill. Wide World Photos.

tional conference to draft an official charter. In April half-a-hundred nations from Europe, Asia, Africa, and North and South America gathered in San Francisco to formally create the United Nations. The Charter was adopted on June 26, 1945.

The goals of the United Nations are the development of international cooperation in maintaining peace and security, in solving economic and social problems, and in promoting human dignity and freedom. Membership is open to all "peace-loving states" who abide by the obligations imposed by the Charter. The General Assembly, the representative body, meets annually in September at the U.N. Headquarters in New York, and special sessions may be called upon request of a majority of the members. Each state, regardless of size or power, has one vote. Action on major questions concerning international peace, or admitting new members, requires a two-thirds vote of the membership; a majority decides routine and minor questions. The General Assembly may discuss any matter which lies within the scope of the Charter, and make recommendations to member states and to the Security Council. As membership increased, these recommendations began to carry greater weight.

In the early days of the U.N. the Security Council dominated the organization. There the United States, Russia, England, France, and China (the Nationalists until 1971, the People's Republic since) as permanent members, each had veto powers on important issues, which tended to paralyze the Council's ability to act, and prevented significant action against any of the five. Therefore, although the Charter provided for six (later ten) members to be elected to the Council by the Assembly, the five permanent members effectively controlled the organization. More recently, however, the General Assembly has begun to act more forcefully, as new nations joined and began collaborating to offset the strength of the great powers. The collective votes of these new members have, in the last decade, created a new power bloc which often opposes the interests of the superpowers.

• The U.N.: Failures and Successes

The U.N. holds no authority over the sovereign rights of its members, and the Charter expressly forbids any intervention in a nation's internal affairs. These limitations severely restrict the U.N.'s jurisdiction, for, while the Charter obliges members to solve problems by peaceful means, it provides no method of forcing a state to abide by the obligation. Although members are required to furnish military assistance when necessity demands, the U.N. has no permanent military force under its own command. The absence of an international police force severely limits the ability of the U.N. to insure peaceful settlement of disputes quickly, but the Military Staff Committee has put together special forces for use in crises in Africa, Cyprus, and the Middle East. These precedents could ultimately evolve into the creation of an effective international security agency.

Joseph Stalin, with Nikita Krushchev in the background. Wide World Photos.

Although the U.N. has not been able to achieve its stated purpose of maintaining world peace and security, it has done outstanding work in other areas. The Economic and Social Council, working through a number of subsidiary agencies such as the United Nations Educational, Scientific, and Cultural Organization (UNESCO) and the World Health Organization (WHO), seek to produce economic and social progress in the underdeveloped nations. These agencies have scored noteworthy achievements in combatting illiteracy, controlling disease, improving communications and furthering economic development.

Despite its limitations, the United Nations represents a major step toward international cooperation. Unquestionably, both the advanced nations and the world's new states support it with enthusiasm as a forum in which world problems of every sort can be openly discussed. But, at the same time that the world searched for security through the creation and growth of the United Nations, the breakdown in relations between the superpowers made that hope more elusive than ever. Even before the Second World War ended, the alliance between Russia and the United States deteriorated and produced a new kind of conflict, a prolonged state of political and military tension and rivalry short of full-scale armed combat.

• From Coalition to Cold War

At the Yalta Conference in 1945 Stalin bluntly insisted on Russian domination of Eastern Europe. Since Russia had borne the brunt of the fighting against the Germans in that area, and since her continued assistance was essential to Germany's defeat, Roosevelt and Churchill suppressed their doubts regarding Russia's promises and tacitly acceded to most of her demands. The three leaders agreed to divide Germany into four zones, occupied by British, French, American, and Russian troops. Berlin was to be similarly divided, although it lay within the boundaries of the Russian occupation zone. Roosevelt and Churchill recognized the existing communist governments in eastern Europe, and did not examine too closely the terms "democratic" and "free elections" promised for other east European countries.

Later in 1945, after Roosevelt's death and Churchill's defeat as England's Prime Minister, another Big Three conference met at Potsdam. This time Harry Truman, the new President of the United States, and Clement Attlee, England's new Prime Minister, met with Stalin. By this time it was evident that the swords were drawn between Russia and the West. The difference in peace aims became so sharp that little agreement between the powers could be reached, except in regard to Germany. The three statesmen did agree that Germany should be demilitarized and deprived of any capacity to wage future wars, that she should pay reparations, that the Nazis should be removed from all positions of influence, and that German war criminals should be punished. During and after Potsdam the relations between East and West quickly deteriorated.

In 1946 the great war-time leader, Winston Churchill, speaking in Fulton, Missouri, said that "From Stettin in the Baltic to Trieste in the Adriatic an iron curtain has descended across the continent." Events proved him right, and the iron curtain marked the line between two drastically different ideologies which quickly became involved in the Cold War to determine which ideology would establish world hegemony. The struggle centered at first in Germany. Russia feared that Germany might again recover from military defeat, as she had after World War I, and again conquer Europe. From such a base she could once more attack Russia. Stalin, therefore, determined that Russia must retain absolute control over all of eastern Europe as a buffer zone, and if possible, gain control over Germany itself. Western European and American statesmen feared Russian control over Germany. From there she could easily dominate all of Europe, especially since France and Italy both already had communists in their governments.

• The Federal Republic of Germany

As recently as the Potsdam meeting the assumption had been that after a period of denazification, reparations payments, and firm evidence that she was no longer dangerous, Germany would be reunited into a single sovereign state. Such was not to be. From the beginning of four-power control Russian policy aimed at using her position to weaken Germany, and to establish a communist state. This policy reached its peak when, in 1948, the Russians closed all land approaches to Berlin. Instead of yielding to the Russian threat, the United States and Great Britain responded with the Berlin "airlift," supplying the needs of the western sector by air for nearly a full year. In fact, Russian intransigence and a continuing economic crisis convinced the western powers that they must unite their three zones in West Germany into a single economic and political unit, and in May, 1949, they handed over most of the responsibility of government to a newly created state, the Federal Republic of Germany, which comprised all of Germany except the Russian zone. The Basic Law (Constitution) provided for a two-house legislature, the Bundesrat (upper house, representing the German states), and the Bundestag (lower house, elected by universal suffrage at age 21, representing the people). Executive power rested in the Chancellor and Cabinet. They were made responsible to the Bundestag, but could not be overturned unless their successors could take over immediate responsibility.

The first elections established Konrad Adenauer as Chancellor, a position he held strongly until 1963. West Germany owes much of its fantastic rebuilding and its present economic success and political stability to Adenauer, who concentrated his efforts on establishing working relationships with other western governments, and especially that of France. He supported every effort to bring Europe closer to unity, and, since Germany was disarmed and had no military expenditures, she quickly rebuilt a strong economy.

• The German Democratic Republic

During the same year in which the Federal Republic was created by the western powers, Russia sponsored the formation of a satellite state in her zone of Germany. Called the German Democratic Republic, the new state was patterned on the Russian system, strongly centralized, and required to take orders from Russia, especially after an abortive revolt in 1953, which was harshly suppressed by the Russian army.

Such constant repression in the East, combined with a weak economy, caused many East Germans to leave the German Democratic Republic in the hope of finding a happier life in West Germany. This constant loss of manpower, and especially skilled labor and the educated classes, threatened the East German economy. In 1961, with Russian permission, East Germany built a wall across the entire city of Berlin and shot anyone who attempted to cross it. Gradually the East German economy improved, as the new state established trade relations with other states in eastern Europe and with Russia. In 1972 a formal treaty was signed between East and West Germany which marked acceptance by both sides of the continuing division of the former nation state.

• Soviet Eastern Europe

In the first three years after the war Russia, with the help of local communists, established "People's Republics" in eight countries in eastern Europe. Poland, Hungary, Czechoslovakia, East Germany, Bulgaria, Rumania, Albania, and Yugoslavia accepted dominance, although Yugoslavia later defected. In all of these states the Russian army had been recognized as the liberator from Nazi occupation and tyranny. Roosevelt and Churchill had officially recognized the area as Russia's sphere of influence, and merely satisfied themselves that Stalin would adhere to the democratic process in recreating the governments of these states. The belief was a delusion. Although the Russians allowed parliamentary processes to remain in existence for a few years, by the end of the decade the last vestiges of democracy had disappeared from eastern Europe.

Several factors contributed to Russia's victory over the eastern European nations: the economic and military weakness of small states devastated by war; vast inequities in the existing economic and social orders; the strength of local communist organizations which had gained support by leading the resistance against the Nazis; and the direct military and economic intervention of the Soviet Union. In most instances, communist leaders obtained key positions in the post-war governments. Once in positions of authority, the communists increased infiltration and directed policy until they were ready to assume domination. Only after they had forced the leading non-communists out of government and sufficiently usurped enough power to insure success did they openly assert control. The establishment of the Soviet sphere was thus by no means an unquestioned power-play of the Russian army. Instead, the foundations of freedom were crumbled from within, gradually enough to hold western intervention at bay.

• Poland, Hungary, Czechoslovakia

In 1944 communists in Poland announced the establishment of the Provisional National Government of the Polish Republic, which immediately received Russian recognition. The Polish government-in-exile, backed by Great Britain and the United States, refused to recognize the legality of the Polish communist government, and the issue came into discussion at the Yalta Conference. There it was decided that the two governments should coalesce, and hold new elections, with universal suffrage and protected voting privileges.

When the elections were finally held in 1947, terror, fraud, and violence insured the success of the communist forces. Purges ensued, in which non-communists and deviant party members fled or were killed or imprisoned, and Poland moved rapidly into totalitarian dictatorship, allowing no internal opposition at all. Following the Soviet model, the new government of the Polish People's Republic began the transformation of Poland from an agricultural to an industrial state.

In Hungary the government formed in 1944, called the Hungarian National Independence Front, was dominated by communists. The general elections in 1945, however, resulted in a coalition victory for the parties of the more moderate center. The monarchy was abolished, and a republic proclaimed. But anti-government elements fomented discord, until, in 1947, new elections which disfranchised some 6 percent of the electorate increased communist representation. Rapidly thereafter the non-communist parties were either disbanded or destroyed, until by 1949 the communists had obtained full control of the government and the country. In February, 1949, the People's Republic of Hungary was proclaimed. Vigorous efforts to collectivize agriculture and increase industry created discontent with the regime, but Russian support prevented serious revolt.

By 1948 Czechoslovakia had fallen to communist control. Factionalism within the state weakened the post-war National Front government, which struggled to reconstruct the economy along socialist lines but at the same time to maintain a compromise with western democratic principles. Cold War antagonisms, however, undermined Czechoslovakia's attempt to straddle the fence between East and West. Russia insisted that the Czechs refuse Marshall Plan aid, desperately needed to restore her economy, and, after 1947, launched a communist attempt to obtain governmental control of the state. Infiltrating the military, the police, and the communications media, the communists acquired a parliamentary majority and ultimately dominated the cabinet. Once in control, they quickly destroyed the political and intellectual freedoms protected by the post-war government. Jan Masaryk, the son of Czechoslovakia's first President and a leader of Czechoslovakian liberalism, committed suicide under extremely suspicious circumstances. In the ensuing years the government moved firmly into the Soviet orbit and increasingly tightened its grasp on Czechoslovakian society.

- ## Rumania, Bulgaria, and Albania

In Rumania a communist-dominated government, established in 1945, retained token participation from other parties until 1947. In that year, however, it moved openly to squash all opposition. In October, after the leaders of the Peasant and Liberal Parties were denounced and tried as traitors, the People's Republic of Rumania was proclaimed. In 1948 a new constitution established a severely repressive soviet-type governmental system, and another eastern state moved firmly into the Soviet bloc.

The Bulgarian People's Republic was established in 1946 and by 1948 the communist regime was firmly consolidated. As in the neighboring eastern states, rapid social and economic transformation followed. By 1956, 90 percent of all peasants had been forced into collective farms, and succeeding Five-Year Plans expedited industrialization.

Communist-controlled forces in Albania emerged victorious from a civil war in 1945 and in 1946 turned the country from a monarchy into an undisguised communist republic. Confiscation and redistribution of the land accompanied nationalization of industry. Ruthlessly pursuing socialization of the economy, the Albanian government demonstrated a brutality remarkable even in the Soviet camp. Economic difficulties with Russia caused friction between the two countries, however, and after 1960 dissension between them intensified into an open rift.

• The Soviet Bloc

As in the Soviet Union, real authority in the People's Republics of eastern Europe rested in the Communist Party. New constitutions provided for one-party control of all institutions and placed the economy under the direction of the state. Each of the new regimes launched industrialization programs aimed at transforming their previously agrarian societies into industrial states. A Soviet-controlled organization called Cominform (Communist Information Bureau) coordinated policy among the communist states and a military alliance under the Warsaw Pact provided a common defense system. The Soviet Union enjoyed economic as well as military advantages from her domination of Eastern Europe. The states of that area not only provided Russia with raw materials and markets on her own terms, but paid reparations to Russia at the same time. Moreover, the satellites of eastern Europe formed a ring of buffer states between Russia and the West — a strategic protection of immense significance to the Soviet Union.

But not everyone was happy with the new regimes. Opposition arose from independent peasant landowners who resisted nationalization of agriculture, and forced industrialization created strains as well, necessitating severe police methods to maintain order. The Churches resisted fiercely, causing the governments to repress religion and to persecute such high-ranking church leaders as Cardinal Mindszenty in Hungary and Cardinal Wyszynski in Poland. The imposition of Russian culture aroused local nationalism. A series of revolts culminated in 1956, when open revolt in Poland and Hungary required direct Soviet military intervention. The Russians, however, had the will to act quickly and with brutal thoroughness and brought the native populations to heel. Lenin's belief that imperialism was the last stage of decadent capitalism had been tossed aside. Russia introduced the world to a new and virulent variety of imperialism, and the horrors of earlier European colonialism were more than matched by the Russians as they exploited eastern Europeans, hammering down age-old cultures, traditions, and social arrangements. Totalitarian controls turned even Czechoslovakia, one of the most industrially advanced and democratic states in the world before the Nazi take-over, into a drab colony of Russia, where individual freedom and human dignity were impossible of achievement.

• Non-Soviet Eastern Europe

The Russian leadership expected to control all of eastern Europe after 1945, but they were foiled in Finland, Austria, and Greece, and Yugoslavia later withdrew its allegiance. Finland chose to resist being incorporated into the Soviet Bloc, and Russia did not make an issue of it because of the danger that if Russia attacked Finland, Sweden's fear would drive her into the western alliance. Besides, Russia had already gained most of what she wanted from Finland in a series of post-war treaties.

In Austria the two major political parties wisely chose to cooperate against Russian dominance instead of fighting each other. The Socialists and the People's Party formed a coalition which was so strong and so effective that it provided the country with its government and administration for an entire generation. Much of the economy was nationalized and even that which remained in private hands came under strong centralized control. By 1955 Austria regained full sovereignty by the Austrian State Treaty, which committed her to a neutral position in the Cold War and which clearly stated that Austria could never become a part of Germany. The Austrian economy quickly recovered. By trading with both East and West, the Austrians raised their standard of living to levels prevalent in the rest of free Europe.

Greece experienced a vicious civil war between communists and non-communists after the expulsion of the German invaders, despite the establishment of a democratically-elected government in 1946. England and the United States supported the government, while Russia's satellites in the area supplied and protected the communist insurgents, which had considerable success until American assistance became too great, and until Yugoslavia cut her ties with Moscow and ceased supporting the communists. Finally the non-communists won a victory, but since that time politics in Greece have been notably unstable. Today, a pro-Western, moderate, democratic government rules Greece and seems to have won the support of the majority of people.

Yugoslavia's defection particularly surprised the Russians, and introduced the idea of "national communism," as opposed to "monolithic communism." When the Cominform attempted to enforce Russian policies and control over Yugoslavia, Marshal Tito, the beloved communist dictator and World War II hero of the resistance, balked. Stalin, failing to understand the strength of nationalism, tried coercion. But even strong non-communists supported Tito against all Russian efforts to subordinate Yugoslavia. Hoping to find an ally, and looking for propaganda advantages, the western states provided Tito with arms and money, and the Yugoslav state gradually established an independent existence. Tito remained firmly communist in his domestic policies and completely neutral in the Cold War diplomacy.

● The Truman Doctrine

Russia's imperialism and her refusal to permit the development of democratic institutions in the eastern European countries caused a strong reaction against her in England and the United States. The British, responsible for restoring Greek institutions after the Germans had been pushed out in 1944, found themselves involved in a civil war in which the guerillas were supplied by Russia's satellites, and by 1947 were too exhausted to handle the rapidly deteriorating situation. At the same time Russia, by demanding concessions from Turkey, indicated that she planned to take over that country. Here, too, England's support proved too much for her own economy. In 1947 the British government informed the United States that she could no longer carry the burden, and President Harry Truman responded to the situation by asking Congress for funds to permit the United States to intervene. In his speech he expressed the belief that ". . . it must be the policy of the United States to support free peoples who are resisting attempted subjugation by armed minorities or by outside pressures." Congress promptly gave the President the necessary legislation, and established what came to be known as the Truman Doctrine: that the United States would give military and economic support to defend non-communist countries against internal and external enemies.

● European Economic Integration

The Truman Doctrine was followed almost immediately by the Marshall Plan. Secretary of State George Marshall, arguing that "Our policy is directed not against any country or doctrine but against hunger, poverty, desperation and chaos," proposed to use American money to revitalize the economies of the European states. The Marshall Plan arose from the belief that communism spread quickly in areas of economic distress. In order to make efficient use of Marshall Plan aid, the interested governments created the Organization for European Economic Cooperation (OEEC), which directed the use of some $12,000,000,000 in U.S. funds in the next five years. This cooperation led naturally to Point 4 of President Truman's inaugural address in 1949, and to the Point 4 Program to provide economic assistance to the former colonial areas of the world.

The Marshall Plan had a profoundly beneficial effect on the European economies and governments. Recognizing that cooperation among themselves would facilitate restoration, the European governments, through OEEC, reduced tariff barriers and deliberately began a policy of integrating the economies of most of the western European states. The combination of American assistance and economic cooperation produced an amazing prosperity where there had been nothing but devastation, hopelessness, and economic chaos. Although the United States had not excluded eastern Europe from receiving Marshall Plan aid, Russia forbade her satellites to participate, thus increasing the gap between the forces on each side of the iron curtain.

The obvious successes of supra-national organization and planning, using Marshall Plan money, led European leadership gradually to transform OEEC into an organization for long-range European cooperation even without American assistance. By 1951 France, West Germany, and Italy joined the Benelux countries (*Be*lgium, *Ne*therlands, *Lux*emburg) in a new six-nation European Coal and Steel Community, which was designed to pool resources and markets in these two products. Again, success led to a broadening of cooperation. In 1955 the same six countries signed an agreement which established the European Economic Community (EEC), or Common Market. The purposes included the ultimate creation of a tariff-free area in western Europe, and while there were lots of problems to solve before that goal had been achieved, the European leaders genuinely recognized that such cooperation was essential.

Other European states soon felt the effects of the EEC on their economies, and, being excluded from membership, formed the European Free Trade Association (EFTA). The seven member states (Austria, Denmark, England, Norway, Portugal, Sweden, Switzerland) set about reducing tariffs, but did not attempt extensive economic integration, and the Outer Seven was less successful than the Inner Six. Since 1969 most of non-communist Europe has been accepted into the EEC. EEC and

Europe-1973

- European Economic Community (Common Market)
- Communist Countries
- "Iron Curtain"
- ① Independent of the Soviet Union
- ② Aligned with Communist China

EFTA now have mutual members, and others may join. Workers already can move easily throughout the Community and social security benefits can be transferred from any member state to a worker's home country. From such beginnings political unity may grow.

● NATO

Increasing prosperity alone could not dismiss the fear of Russia in the minds of Europeans. Military cooperation, as well as economic, was required. Some steps had been taken in this direction by 1948, but it was only with the American adoption of the containment policy that a significant structure was created. The containment policy proceeded from the assumption that Russia's imperialism could be stopped by "adroit and vigilant application of counter-force. . ." every time and every place Russia attempted to move out of the area she already controlled. With such a policy it was necessary to have highly mobile troops strategically located, and to have Russia fully aware of the capability of containment. In 1949, therefore, the United States and Canada joined most of the western European states in the North Atlantic Treaty Organization (NATO). NATO, like EEC, was based on close cooperation among the European states, and required all members to integrate their military planning for common defense. An attack on one member would be looked upon as an attack on all members, and NATO would respond accordingly. American support for NATO responsibilities added economic support to Marshall Plan aid, and the added security contributed to Europe's economic recovery.

• Japan's Recovery

While a resurgent western Europe moved toward economic integration and corporate security to curb the threat of the Soviet menace, the spread of revolutionary communism to the non-European world accelerated the buildup of Cold War tensions. As Europe's weakness became apparent immediately after the war, local communist forces grew strong in most of Asia. They argued for national self-determination, exclusion of foreign oppression, and major land reforms. Japan's wartime occupation of most of southeast Asia bred nationalism in those lands, and her early victories against the United States convinced many Asians that they, too, could end their old subservience to western dominance.

The association of communist nationalists with anti-colonialism frightened the American government and caused a drastic revision of original plans for the occupation of Japan. The occupying forces chose to rule through the established government, which it reformed along democratic lines, and this avoided much of the lasting bitterness usually associated with occupation of defeated countries. Vast American economic assistance (six billion dollars in a dozen years) enabled Japanese industry to develop widespread economic prosperity as it produced for the growing markets in the Far East.

While the United States and other industrial powers devoted ever-greater portions of their economies to the military in pursuit of Cold War aims, Japan, unhindered by any military expenditures, became a major industrial power and began to challenge even the home markets of its industrial competitors. In 1968 Japan by-passed West Germany to become the third-ranking industrial power in the world. Although her growing prosperity invalidated American fears that Japan would succumb to communism, in 1949 a revolution in China turned the largest nation in the Far East into the communist camp.

• The Communist Revolution in China

Chinese nationalism regenerated in the first decade of the century – in 1911 a republican revolution, led by Sun Yat-sen, brought the Kuomintang, or Chinese Nationalist Party, into power. But Sun's political successor, Chiang Kai-shek, failed to develop centralized authority sufficient to solve China's economic ills. An enduring feudal aristocracy resisted land reform and governmental corruption undermined support of the Kuomintang. Led by Mao Tse-tung, Chinese communists won the allegiance of the rural disinherited, disenchanted nationalists and humanitarian intellectuals. Having nothing to defend, the Chinese peasants did not oppose the communists, who promised to raise their standard of living. Of 450 million Chinese, only a handful actively participated in the Civil War, but as the communists took over a region the land-hungry peasants joined in revolt against the established authorities. In 1949 Chiang Kai-shek and a few devoted followers were driven to the island of Formosa (Taiwan) off the coast of China, where he established authoritarian control with the support of the United States. Despite the overwhelming evidence that he had no real chance of successfully returning to power in China, Chiang continued to claim legitimate authority over the mainland.

On October 1, 1949, the communists announced the establishment of the People's Republic of China. Sweeping land reform drew the support of the peasants and the government quickly established sufficient strength to launch a ruthless program of economic modernization without regard to cost in human life. Striking advances were made through five year plans which concentrated on agricultural collectivization and the development of basic industrial facilities. Before the end of the 1950s, Mao and his lieutenants had effected a radical transformation of Chinese society.

Russia immediately recognized the Chinese communist government and in 1950 signed a thirty-year treaty of friendship with the Red Chinese, but ideological differences soon caused a rift between the two. Communist China had no intention of becoming a satellite of the U.S.S.R. Adopting a fiercely militant revolutionary doctrine, the Chinese rejected the concept of peaceful co-existence and demonstrated a determination to control Asia which led to territorial clashes with the Soviet Union along their mutual borders. The Sino-Soviet split had wide-ranging repercussions as the east

European countries recognized a possible alternative to Russian dominance and a potential alternative leadership. Following the communist victory over mainland China, Mao Tse-tung emerged as a dynamic revisionist of communist theory, particularly influential in Europe and in the Third World. He deviated from orthodox Marxism by placing the peasants in the center of the revolutionary endeavor and thereby making the communist philosophy applicable in the world's pre-modern, pre-industrial areas. Mao remained a dominant figure in China and in world communism until his death in 1976.

The United States refused to recognize the Chinese communist government, insisting that Chiang Kai-shek and the Nationalists were the rightful authority. Consequently, the U.S. signed a mutual defense treaty with the exiled government on Formosa and followed it with military and economic assistance. Defending Chiang's claim to legitimacy, the U.S. also took the lead in blocking Red China's admission to the United Nations until 1971.

• The Korean Conflict

The Chinese revolution intensified American fears of communist expansion and caused an extension of the containment policy to include the Far East as well as Europe. When communist forces invaded South Korea in June, 1950, the United States resorted to direct military intervention to prevent a Communist take-over.

A former Japanese colony, Korea was divided along the 38th parallel at the Potsdam Conference, with the Soviets occupying the northern region and the Americans the southern. In 1948 the South Koreans established the Republic of Korea; North Korea responded by announcing the formation of the People's Democratic Republic of Korea. Both claimed sovereignty over the entire country. When the Soviet and American occupying forces withdrew in 1949, the crisis between the rival governments mounted. In June, 1950, a North Korean army suddenly crossed the 38th parallel and invaded South Korea. The United States immediately appealed to the United Nations, which called on U.N. members to aid in defending South Korea from communist aggression. Since the U.S.S.R. had temporarily withdrawn from the organization to protest the refusal to admit Red China to membership, the Soviets could not block the action. Fifteen nations sent forces into Korea, but Americans provided the predominant military resistance. The war became chiefly an American struggle against the North Korean communists, supported by about 200,000 Chinese.

It ended in a stalemate. Frustrating negotiations dragged on for two years, and finally produced, in July, 1953, an armistice which retained the division of the country. The conflict, which ended with neither victors nor vanquished, resulted only in the devastation of Korean territory, the death of 3,000,000 Koreans and more than 100,000 Americans. It did, however, mark the United States as the world's police force against communism. Europe and the anti-communist factions throughout the world adopted a complacent assurance that Americans would and could contain communist aggression.

• The End of Bipolarity

Chinese aggrandizement provoked attempts to create regional security organizations in Asia patterned on the European NATO alliance. In September, 1954, the United States, England, France, Australia, New Zealand, Pakistan, the Philippines, and Thailand signed the Manila Pact, which provided for the formation of the Southeast Asia Treaty Organization. SEATO completed the division of the globe into rival blocs. Cold War competition had expanded to include the entire world.

But rapidly accelerating events were already undermining the foundations of bipolar domination. By 1954 both Russia and the United States had stockpiled sufficient nuclear weapons to destroy life on the globe. The military balance forced the conclusion that neither could emerge victorious from a nuclear confrontation — only annihilation would result. Recognition of the undeniable ecological devastation resulting from continued testing exerted further pressure to end the suicidal armaments race and produced negotiations which ultimately resulted in the nuclear test-ban treaty of 1963.

Simultaneously, nationalism operated to weaken the ties between the superpowers and their previously submissive allies. The power of the United States and Russia began to decline relative to the growing strength and restiveness of the rest of the world. A new climate became apparent as the world entered an era of global politics, with long range economic, political and social repercussions within the European community.

22

The Emerging Nations in the Contemporary Era

ONE OF THE MOST striking characteristics of the contemporary period is a shift in the focus of history from a European to a global perspective. For more than 400 years Europe dominated the historical stage. The last decades of the nineteenth century witnessed the rapid exportation of European authority to all corners of the globe. Europe's collapse in the twentieth century brought in its wake the disintegration of European world hegemony. Beginning after World War I and accelerating rapidly after World War II, a revolt against European domination and a strong assertion of national self-determination in the industrially under-developed nations swept the globe, crumbling the old colonial empires, and challenging the economic leadership of the industrially advanced nations.

Europe's loss of economic, political, and military power began a new era of world politics. Russia and the United States, the two superpowers, vied for supremacy, each pursuing the allegiance of the rest of the world. Bipolarity dominated world politics for over a decade, but by the 1960s a new power structure was clearly recognizable. It rested on a regenerated Europe and a rʒw bloc of developing nations in Asia, Africa, and Latin America, called the "Third World." By 1970 this shifting coalition held the balance in the conflict between the Russian and American superpowers. The breakup of Europe's colonial empires generated the Third World bloc.

• The Twilight of Empire

Although economic necessities had undeniably encouraged the acquisition of empire, Europe's imperialistic motivations included a complex mixture of political and economic domination and paternalism. The "White Man's Burden" dictated an inculcation of western ideas and mores into native cultures and left a mixed heritage in the colonial areas. Lord Curzon, England's Viceroy in India (1899-1905), articulated the attitudes of the European masters when he described empire as the means of service to mankind as well as the key to glory and wealth. And imperialism did indeed spread Europe's advanced cultural concepts to the less highly developed areas of the globe. In most European colonies westernized elites, educated in European schools, absorbed the ideas of popular sovereignty, individualism, and self-determination asserted so vigorously by their imperial masters. Moreover, they determined to industrialize and modernize their homelands in order to share the material comforts of twentieth-century society. This urge quickened after Russia's rapid industrialization in the 1930s showed the way. Imperialism consequently sowed the seeds of its own destruction — it awakened slumbering societies to the benefits of modernization and at the same time, because of its frequently harsh economic demands, created a determination to throw off the yoke of foreign domination.

After 1945 the colonial empires disintegrated with a rapidity that astonished everyone. England led in relinquishing empire, as she had led in acquiring it — hers was the first of the imperial structures to crumble. Although a strong imperialistic wing still existed in the British Conservative Party, Labour grasped control in the immediate post-war years and spurred imperial disintegration. Labour insisted that all people, of whatever race or color, had an equal right to freedom and national sovereignty. The British Commonwealth policy, instituted with the Statute of Westminister in 1931, facilitated England's withdrawal from empire. It declared that the dominions were autonomous states, equal in status with each other and with Great Britain, freely associated in common allegiance to the crown in the Commonwealth of Nations. Although the Commonwealth idea was adopted specifically in regard to Canada and Australia — western nations populated with whites — it established a precedent which later included non-western colonies as England considered them capable of self-rule.

France, more reluctant to give up her colonial possessions, pursued an ambivalent course. Although imperialism remained strong in conservative segments of the French population, the Second World War necessitated changes in France's colonial policies. A French Union preserved the French possessions and dominance from Paris, but allowed limited self-government and colonial representation in the French Parliament. Unlike the British Commonwealth, the French Union was a weak and unsatisfactory structure from the beginning and never attained viability. Belgium, the Netherlands, and Portugal, the remaining imperial powers, tried desperately but unsuccessfully to hold on to their colonies.

● India

The challenge to European control began in Asia. China's nationalist revolution in the first decade of the twentieth century initiated a drive toward independence which gained impetus in Asia in the inter-war period. India took the lead in discarding imperial rule.

Spurred by the leadership of Mohandas Gandhi, an ascetic, western-educated champion of Indian freedom, Indian demands for self-government began before World War I. Gandhi urged a policy of passive resistance, non-violence, and civil disobedience to British rule. Under pressure from Gandhi and his fellow nationalists, the British passed the Government of India Act in 1919, designed to train the Indian population toward independence. The Act established a parliament and elective provincial legislative councils. Limited self-rule did not satisfy the demands of the nationalists, however, and disorder increased. Religious and cultural differences between Hindus and Moslems complicated the situation and despite Gandhi's insistence on non-violence, terrorist acts frequently occurred. The Moslem League, a political party which opposed Gandhi's Hindu Congress Party, rejected co-existence with the Hindu majority and militantly insisted on partition of the territory and the creation of a separate Moslem state. Since complete division of the inextricably intermingled populations could not be realized, the British, also unwilling to lose the economic benefits of exploitation, resisted the demands for partition.

In 1940 Indian nationalists, now led by Jawaharlal Nehru, an English-educated Indian aristocrat, rejected a British offer of semi-autonomy, belligerently insisting on full independence. As Hindu-Moslem differences continued to cause disturbances and riots the British reluctantly recognized that partition was inevitable. In 1947 England granted independent dominion status to India, the predominantly Hindu area, and to a new state, Pakistan, formed of the severed Moslem territories. Both republics became Commonwealth members.

• Independence and After

Independence and partition failed to resolve the religious and civil discord. Following England's withdrawal, violent civil wars broke out in India and Pakistan, as minorities clashed with ruling majorities. Territorial disputes further embittered relations between the two countries, as both claimed the province of Kashmir. Neither could quell the civil turmoil nor resolve the external conflict. At the same time, both nations struggled to solve monumental social and economic problems.

Modernization in India requires more than the development of industrial facilities and improved methods of agriculture. India has a population of more than 600 million, most of them underfed, illiterate, and with archaic religious and cultural traditions. In his attempt to advance the drive toward modernization, Nehru, India's Prime Minister from 1947 to 1964, utilized assistance in foreign aid from both the United States and Russia. Nehru's policy of non-alignment in the ideological struggle between the super-powers established a model emulated by most of the other Third World States.

Pakistan's division into two segments complicated her efforts to modernize. East and West Pakistan were separated by a thousand miles, united only by a common religion and rent with linguistic and cultural differences. Pakistani leadership could not cement the two. In 1971 dissension erupted into civil war and resulted in further fragmentation. East Pakistan announced its independence as a new state, and took the name of Bangladesh. Hindu minorities fled into India, creating a staggering refugee problem. Thousands starved to death, and the influx imposed a heavy burden on India's already over-taxed economy.

In other areas of Asia new states arose in profusion. The British granted independence to Burma and Ceylon in 1948, and belatedly to Malaya in 1957 after a long war against communist guerilla forces. The United States, fulfilling a pre-war promise, granted independence to the Philippines in 1946. In 1949 after four years of bloody conflict, the Dutch finally retreated from Indonesia, and a federal republic was created.

In the years since independence each of these states has struggled to improve living conditions for populations which still live largely in a medieval world. Entrenched elites have resisted land redistribution and maintained a stranglehold on government machinery which has greatly hindered progress. The disinherited segments of these Asian populations have not acquiesced easily in socio-economic stagnation. Their demands for a share of the wealth have encouraged the development of communist cadres which seek to undermine the established governments. Government corruption and refusal to reform have fed ever increasing numbers of normally quiescent peasants into the ranks of revolutionary movements seeking economic improvement. This characteristic pattern in the Asian world was most insistently demonstrated in French Indo-China, which fragmented after the war into Vietnam, Cambodia and Laos.

• Vietnam

During World War II the French possession in Vietnam became the seat of a complicated power struggle between the French, the Japanese, and the natives, led by Ho Chi Minh, a Communist-trained nationalist who was determined to establish an independent native republic. When the French attempted to re-establish control over the area after the war, Ho and his insurgents, the Vietminh, resisted fiercely. In 1946 the French granted Vietnam semi-autonomy within the French Union, but the nationalist rebellion continued. Because of the Vietminh's communist orientation, the French refused to accede to the increasingly insistent Vietnamese demands for full independence. The struggle became full-scale war in 1946.

The war in Indo-China continued for eight years, becoming an interminable conflict which drained France's already depleted resources, and was enormously unpopular with the French people. In 1949 the Soviet Union and the new communist Chinese government recognized Ho's Vietminh regime as the legitimate government in Vietnam. The United States and England recognized Vietnam and the neighboring French Protectorates of Laos and Cambodia as member states of the French Union, and the United States poured vast economic aid into the French military effort. But nothing could stem the tide of nationalism.

From 1950 to 1954 Ho broadened his base of popular support and stepped up guerilla tactics. The absorption of French energies in the Vietnamese war allowed Laos and Cambodia to demand and receive greater sovereignty over their own affairs, thus preventing the outbreak of open conflict in those areas. In 1954, after a disastrous defeat at Dien Bien Phu, the French admitted their inability to continue the struggle and withdrew from Vietnam.

The fall of Dien Bien Phu marked the end of French imperialist control in southeast Asia. The Geneva Conference in 1954 partitioned Vietnam along the seventeenth parallel. The Communist Democratic Republic of Vietnam, led by Ho Chi Minh, was established in the North, and the Nationalist Republic of Vietnam in the South. Laos and Cambodia acquired full independence.

But the civil war in Vietnam continued after partition. Determined to unite the country under his leadership, Ho Chi Minh proclaimed a Fatherland Front and urged the South Vietnamese government to cooperate in unification, but the ruler of South Vietnam, Ngo Dinh Diem, refused to negotiate. Diem, a Catholic, issued a constitution and promised elections in South Vietnam, but assumed dictatorial powers. He received enormous aid from the United States because of his declared anti-communism, but was unable to win the support of his own people who charged him with religious persecution and vehemently protested his religious policies. Buddhist monks led the rebellion, sometimes resorting to such extreme protests as self-immolation. As Diem continued to resist demands for change, the civil war intensified, and the local communist forces, the National Liberation Front (NLF), gained more and more adherents.

• U.S. Intervention

The United States, having adopted the "Domino Theory" — a belief that the fall of one state to communism would inevitably result in the fall of all — chose to take France's place in South Vietnam. Gradually it became clear that Ngo Dinh Diem was insupportable and the United States participated in a coup which overthrew his government. Succeeding South Vietnamese governments accepted increasing American economic and military intervention until more than half-a-million American soldiers were fighting the Vietnamese insurgents. While the United States pretended that it was defending freedom and saving civilization from godless communism, the more experienced Europeans realized that much of Ho Chi Minh's support rested on a determined desire for Vietnamese independence from foreign domination. American involvement in Vietnam became the central international event of the decade between 1960 and 1970. Many Americans and most Europeans agonized over the United States' military policies, which resulted in defoliation of the Vietnamese forests, the use of napalm against villagers whose allegiance was uncertain, and the massacre of village populations, including women and small children, such as occurred at My Lai in 1968. As it became increasingly obvious that America's national and vital interests were not threatened by the civil war in Vietnam, increasing numbers of citizens questioned the justification of American involvement in a war which seemed not only imperialistic but interminable as well. As war costs mounted past $400,000,000,000 the

Terrified children fleeing after being burned by a misplaced American napalm bombing. Wide World Photos.

anti-war movement, dominated initially by the young, eventually enlisted the support of many influential leaders. In the presidential election of 1968 the war was a major campaign issue. Promising to withdraw American troops from Vietnam "with all reasonable speed," the Republican candidate, Richard Milhous Nixon, defeated the Democrats who bore the public responsibility for escalating the war.

Nixon proved incapable of speedy withdrawal from Vietnam. His program, called Vietnamization, which included gradually reducing American troop levels, strengthening the Vietnamese Army and negotiating for peace, failed. While American bombing of Vietnam and Cambodia escalated, peace negotiations remained at an impasse until 1973, when an agreement abruptly ended America's participation. As American troops and thousands of Vietnamese refugees left the country in chaotic haste, the insurgents consolidated one of history's most brutal regimes, which imposed forcible resettlement of at least 4,000,000 people. The 1975 victory of the Communists in Cambodia, now re-named Kampuchea, resulted in an equally ruthless social revolution, involving the systematic slaughter of hundreds of thousands.

While most Europeans had vigorously condemned American involvement, many feared that the American withdrawal from the defense against communism in Southeast Asia would also mean ultimate withdrawal from Europe's defense. Europe feared that Vietnamization would be followed by Europeanization, and fears of Russian aggrandizement had not sufficiently abated to face such a prospect with equanimity. Increasing international tensions in the Middle East reinforced Europe's fears for its own security.

• The Middle East

The Ottoman Empire had extended over most of the Arab world, although England and France had established protectorates over portions of the Middle East. Turkish and European domination produced, even before the First World War, an Arab leadership determined to end foreign control and gain national independence. Allied with Germany in the First World War, the Turkish Empire disintegrated after the defeat of the Central Powers. Despite the efforts of Arab nationalists to unite the Arab lands of the Middle East into an independent state, the League of Nations extended European control, granting England and France mandates over Arab territories. Instead of unifying the Arab world, the League of Nations mandates divided it into a number of small, antagonistic states united only in their opposition to foreigners and in their determination to prevent the foundation of a Jewish nation in Palestine.

In 1917 the British government's Balfour Declaration announced that England favored the establishment in Palestine, the historic Jewish homeland now populated with Arabs, of a "national home for the Jewish people," and would support the creation of such a state. The Declaration promised, however, that all civil and religious rights of Arab residents would be protected. Encouraged by the Balfour Declaration, large numbers of Jews, especially from eastern Europe, migrated into Palestine between the wars. Many of the new settlers represented a literate, technically advanced class, imbued with the ideas of democratic socialism.

Tensions grew between the Jewish immigrants and the Palestinian Arabs as the culturally advanced Jews tried to turn economically backward Palestine into a modern nation. Between the wars Palestine developed more rapidly than other Arab regions, but inevitably the Arab people resisted Jewish dominance and the rapid change in their way of life. Clashes between the two groups occurred constantly.

After World War II vast numbers of Europe's surviving Jews poured into Palestine, fleeing the horrors they had endured under the Nazis, and seeking security and protection in a "national home." By 1947 tensions between Arab and Jew had reached such proportions that England decided to withdraw from the area, and asked the United Nations to resolve the problem. When England removed her troops in 1948, however, the U.N. had found no satisfactory solution, and the Jews unilaterally proclaimed the independence and autonomy of the state of Israel as a republic.

- ● Arab-Israeli Conflict

The immediate consequence was war between the Palestinian Arabs and the Israelis, quickly won by the latter because the Arabs were disunited. Nearly a million Palestinian Arabs fled Israel and established themselves in refugee camps in neighboring Arab states where they remain, living in misery and squalor, refusing assimilation, demanding to be restored to their lost home. The camps bred fanatical terrorist groups which intensified Israeli defensiveness. Arab terror tactics had world-wide repercussions as innocent non-Jew and non-Arab people were drawn into the conflict. Arab fanatics hijacked international airplanes and held the passengers as hostages to wring concessions from the Israelis. Bombings of planes and embassies aroused world-wide hostility. In 1972 Arab terrorists violated the traditional neutrality of the Olympic Games in Munich, Germany, and killed several members of the Israeli Olympic team. Such irrational activities have served to harden antagonism to the Arab cause, and to arouse sympathy for the Israelis. Europeans, genuinely distressed by German atrocities and pleased that the Jews had found a home in the Arab world rather than in Europe, tended to side with the Israelis against the Arabs. Arab terrorism strengthened European and American sympathies for the Jewish cause, but the Russian bloc supported the Arabs, supplying military equipment and moral support to the Arab League, a union of the major Arab states dominated by Egypt. The Arab-Israeli conflict thus became of major significance in international politics, and the tension aroused fears that the area would serve as the tinderbox for a new world war. These fears caused the United States, France, and England to agree in 1950 to limit their sales of military equipment to both sides, a decision which angered the nationalists and contributed to a dangerous situation in 1956.

• The Suez Canal Crisis

The Suez Canal Crisis greatly stimulated Arab nationalism, seriously damaged the western alliance, marked the decline of British power and influence in the Middle East, and fostered significant growth of presidential power in the United States at the expense of Congress. In 1954 an Anglo-Egyptian agreement provided for gradual withdrawal of British troops from the Suez Canal Zone, to be completed by 1956. Under the agreement the Suez Canal Company continued to operate the canal and both countries guaranteed freedom of its use to all countries. Egypt granted that in case of attack on any Arab country or Turkey, British troops might return to protect the canal.

The United States had helped in the negotiations, hoping to create a Middle Eastern Treaty Organization (METO) to fill the containment gap between NATO and SEATO. Iraq, Pakistan, Turkey, Iran, and Great Britain joined, but Egypt refused. She wanted weapons to use against Israel, not Russia, and she wanted the leadership of Arab nationalism. Russia saw the opportunity and agreed to swap Russian and Czechoslovakian weapons for Egyptian cotton. Egypt's flirtation with Russia caused the United States and England first to promise huge funding to build the High Aswan Dam in Egypt, then later, when the Egyptians failed to align with the West, to withdraw the funding. Bitterly seeking a way to retaliate, Egypt nationalized the Suez Canal Company in 1956, giving her control over shipping which passed through the canal. But about 60 percent of the oil used in France and England had to pass through the Suez.

Israel, too, worried about Russian arms in Egypt. After a series of conferences failed to impress the Egyptians, France, England, and Israel chose military force. The Israelis attacked Egypt across the Sinai Peninsula, and British and French troops, fully expecting American support, were sent to "protect the canal." But the United States joined Russia in a U.N. General Assembly order to cease fire, and the sending of a U.N. military force to the canal to replace Anglo-French troops in defending the canal. Under heavy world pressure the invaders returned home.

England's humiliation weakened the western alliance, METO lost much of its effectiveness, Egypt took the lead in Arab nationalism, and the U.S. government feared a Russian take-over of the entire area. President Eisenhower requested, and received from Congress in 1957, presidential authority to order U.S. military intervention to secure and protect the territorial integrity of any nation threatened with armed aggression by international communism. Former Secretary of State Dean Acheson suggested that this "Eisenhower Doctrine" amounted to a threat "to fight an enemy that is not going to attack with forces that do not exist to carry out a policy you have not yet decided upon." Egypt was not controlled by international communism. Her goals were the leadership of Arab nationalism and the destruction of Israel. Neither of Egypt's goals has been achieved, and the Eisenhower Doctrine later provided the foundation for the presidential escalation of the war in Vietnam.

Arab and Jewish animosity erupted into war again in 1967. Again Israel's disciplined, highly-trained, well-equipped forces defeated the Arabs and extended Israel's boundaries. In the "Six-Day War" the Israelis awed the world by their easy victory over an Arab army equipped with Russian tanks and airplanes. The Israeli triumph weakened Egyptian leadership, intensified Arab hostility, and exacerbated the crisis. Major foreign powers deplored Israel's action and the United Nations unsuccessfully demanded that she withdraw from the territory she had conquered.

• Underdevelopment in the Arab States

Israel's neighbors could not match her economic achievements. Despite vast mineral resources – the Middle East is one of the world's largest oil-producing areas, second only to North America – wealth has not extended to the masses of the populations. Economic progress in the oil-rich Arab states is seriously retarded by the opposition of dominating elites – tribal shieks, military oligarchies, and native aristocracies – who have subordinated their people's interests to their own in dealing with the oil-using western states. The need for oil and the area's strategic importance sustained vital interest in the area by the United States, Russia, and western Europe. Although the United States has done much to extend education and economic progress in the Arab nations, American support for Israel marks the United States as an enemy in the eyes of Arab statesmen, while Russia supports the Arab cause to provide a buffer zone between the West and Russia. Huge differences in levels of economic, cultural, and social development among the Arab states maintain division in the area and prevent common political action. The key to progress in the Middle East is unification of the Arab states to share technological knowledge, to expand markets, and to stimulate social reform. Egypt has tried to provide leadership for unity, but the Arab countries remain divided. The Arab League, established in 1945 with headquarters in Cairo, has not been able to overcome national self-interest in its member states. Formerly dominated by Egypt's dynamic Gamal Abdul Nasser, the League has effectively harassed Israel, but has not attracted the loyalty of all the Arab states. Nasser's dependence on Soviet technical and financial assistance alienated those nations determined to pursue a neutral policy in the Cold War conflict, and his undisguised desire to assume leadership of the Arab world offended other Mid-East statesmen. His prestige declined after the humiliating Arab defeat in 1967 and since his death in 1970 his successor, Anwar Sadat, has attempted to head Egypt in new directions.

The growing dependence of Western nations on the immense reserves of Middle Eastern oil has given the Arabs an economic weapon of formidable power. Further territorial losses to Israel after the eighteen-day Yom Kippur War in October 1973 heightened Arab awareness of the international political implications of oil and produced the growth of Arab economic cooperation, marked by the sudden power of OPEC (Organization of Petroleum Exporting Countries). The oil embargo which followed the Yom Kippur War and the subsequent sharp rise in the prices of petroleum products caused an energy crisis of major proportions in western Europe. Arab wealth, heavily invested in Western economies, has further complicated the role of the Middle East in world affairs. Unabated Arab-Israeli tensions keep alive the threat of an explosion in the Middle East and underscore the danger of foreign intervention. Although Sadat, the United Nations, OPEC and the United States have all made strenuous efforts to resolve the tensions in the interests of peace, the area has remained one of the world's danger spots.

• Africa

The determination to achieve modern economic comforts through independence and self-determination struck Africa with explosive force. Before the Second World War, four independent nations existed on the African continent; by 1960, 39 nations had emerged. The new African states passionately support the objectives of the Third World bloc: to pursue an independent course in evolving political systems which will serve their own unique needs, and to accelerate economic improvement for their impoverished populations. The nationalist revolution in Africa, however, faces severe internal challenges.

Immediately after the Second World War several African leaders began agitation for independence. Such men as Kwame Nkrumah of the Gold Coast and Jomo Kenyatta of Kenya not only provided leadership for their own people, but served as examples for other African leaders. In the 1950s and 1960s new states emerged from former colonial possessions with bewildering rapidity. Bloody tribal rebellion, violence of an extreme nature, brutal civil war, and territorial fragmentation accompanied

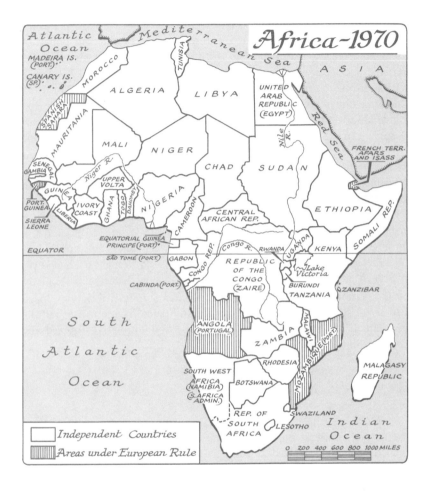

Africa—1970

Independent Countries

Areas under European Rule

independence. In Nigeria in 1967 the Ibo, one of the three dominant tribal groupings, broke away from the state and formed the independent Republic of Biafra. The Nigerians coldheartedly and ruthlessly reunited the nation. A bloody tribal rebellion led by the Mau-Mau in Kenya lasted eight years. After Belgium abruptly broke her ties with the Congo, violence, horror and massacre required United Nations intervention. These events illustrated the enduring force of primitive traditions and patterns, and demonstrated clearly the weakness of African nationalism. Africans had to overcome not only their colonial experience, but perhaps more significantly, the handicaps of centuries of tribal allegiances which counter the movement toward modern nationalism.

In southern Africa white settlers refused to grant native demands for participation in government, and enforced a fierce and rigid policy of subjugation called *apartheid*. The British government demanded that the extreme racial segregation of *apartheid* be dropped, but in 1961 South Africa withdrew from the Commonwealth rather than yield. In 1965 Rhodesia unilaterally proclaimed her independence from British rule and joined South Africa in a fanatical determination to maintain *apartheid*. Despite censure by the United Nations and international economic sanctions, the two south African states defiantly persisted in their determination to keep the non-European population from political participation. The recent Rhodesian offers to share power still remain unacceptable to many blacks.

The French government faced special problems in her territories in northern Africa. Tunisia and Morocco, after years of internal discord and futile efforts by France to resist demands for self-rule, gained independence in 1956. But many French families in Algeria thought of themselves as French citizens and resisted demands for independence led particularly by the National Liberation Front (NLF), and a bloody civil war developed into terroristic tactics both in Algeria and in France. The terrorism and the government's brutal response led to chaos and ultimately toppled the Fourth French Republic.

• The Future in Africa

Most of the new African states attempted to pattern their governments on west European models, with all the institutions instantly created which had evolved in Europe over hundreds of years. They failed to realize that parliamentary democracy requires, for viability, a large degree of willingness to compromise, an educated citizenry, sufficient income to provide leisure time to devote to political and cultural pursuits. None of these requisites characterized the new African states. They have tended to develop into one-party systems, governed by charismatic leaders — native nationalists whose leadership frequently appears demagogic.

The worst of these, exemplified by Uganda's Idi Amin, are savage, self-serving megalomaniacs, who seriously retard hopes of rational evolution in African societies. Africa's challenge is to find consensus between black and white, to leap politically, economically and socially from stone-age cultures to industrialized societies — an arduous task, indeed.

Chaos in Africa has opened it to interference from outside forces. Recently international communism has played a large role on the African continent, with, for example, the direct intervention of Cuba in Angola's civil war. Although Europe and the United States have exercised apprehensive restraint, Cuba in 1978 had as many as 50,000 troops in Africa, supplied with advanced Soviet weapons. The United Nations has not been effective in enforcing a hands-off policy in the seething African nations. Self-determination in Africa faces the most wrenching problems of the century, both internal and external, and the future is darkly seen.

• Latin America

In their growing concern over communism in the Third World, Europe and the United States closely watched developments in Latin America. Despite overwhelming difficulties in overcoming particularism and internal division, many of the nations in Latin America have begun social revolutions and are engaged in widely divergent forms of political experimentation. As the most economically advanced of the Third World regions, its solutions will inevitably serve as models for the contemporary world's emerging states.

Like Russia and the United States, Latin America remained on the periphery of world affairs until the twentieth century. During the Second World War, however, developments there assumed a new significance. The Allied and Axis Powers engaged in vigorous economic competition for the allegiance of the Latin American nations. All except Argentina, which had a pro-fascist government, broke diplomatic relations with the Axis powers before 1943 and strong pressure brought even that country around early in 1945.

After the war the Latin American states faced many of the same political and economic difficulties found in other portions of the Third World. Their efforts to emulate European and American political movements had failed, primarily because of the weakness of their middle classes which tended to support authoritarian dictatorships rather than to lead genuine reform movements.

Grinding poverty, high illiteracy rates, and a medieval social structure contributed to the development of communist groups in Latin America. The 1956 Twentieth Party Congress in Moscow encouraged the idea of "national communism," appealing to hatred of foreign economic domination and the conspicuous wealth of the upper classes. The incredibly poor peasants and workers in Latin America turned to communism as a method of improving their miserable lot. Increasingly radical demands generated fears among the ruling elites, in Europe, and in the United States, of a communist takeover.

Fear of communist advance in the western hemisphere produced the Inter-American Treaty of Reciprocal Assistance in 1947, which provided for collective defense of the American republics against internal as well as external communist threats. This was followed the next year by the Organization of American States which pledged consultation on matters of mutual interest and guaranteed that the United States would not interfere in the domestic or foreign policies of any Latin American state.

• The Cuban Revolution

U.S. policy-makers, however, paid little heed to their own promises, to the obvious distress of even the most anti-communist Latin American leaders. American participation in the disastrous Bay of Pigs episode in 1961 caused grave damage to inter-American relations. Cuba's vicious right-wing dictator, Fulgencio Batista, was overthrown by Fidel Castro in 1959. Castro proclaimed himself a communist, expropriated the property of American citizens, and killed or exiled thousands of his opponents. In April, 1961, Cuban refugees, with assistance from the C.I.A., attempted an invasion to overthrow Castro. The ill-conceived landing at the Bay of Pigs miscarried miserably and the failure of the Cuban population to rise in support of the invading forces indicated that the people largely supported Castro's government.

A year later the Russians began establishing missile bases in Cuba. Washington viewed this practice as a serious threat to American security because from Cuba the missiles could threaten even the northeastern population centers of the United States, and because Russia would have successfully interfered in the American sphere of influence. President John F. Kennedy threatened atomic war unless the Russian missiles were removed immediately, although he agreed at the same time that the United States would not invade Cuba. Russia complied with the demand and the diplomatic victory restored some of the previously lost prestige of the United States.

In an effort to prevent the spread of communism in the Latin American Republics, the United States initiated a series of programs of financial assistance. Congress largely funded the creation of the Inter-American Development Bank in 1959 and 1960, and in 1961 the Kennedy administration launched the ambitious Alliance for Progress, which has poured more than five billion dollars into all the Latin American countries except Cuba. But the economic factors retarding progress in Latin America have not been eradicated. Extractive economies dependent on limited markets, deficiencies in scientific and technological personnel, and lagging inter-regional cooperation maintain social conditions which form breeding grounds for revolutionary doctrines. After more than a century of independence, political maturity in Latin America still proves elusive.

• The Third World Presence in International Affairs

Unquestionably, the nations of the Third World bloc are politically and economically diverse — distinctions rather than similarities prevail. Solidarity is only a semblance. Their impact on international politics has nevertheless radically altered contemporary power alignments. In the United Nations small, poor countries account for a majority of the votes in the General Assembly. Such states as Zambia and Burundi voted with the majority 92 percent of the time in 1972, while the United States increasingly opposed it. The Third World bloc can sometimes, but not always, enforce its will, because the small states lack the clout to make the great powers respond. Brazil's Ambassador to the United States spoke for many Third World leaders when he warned that "the U.N. is becoming irrelevant on matters of peace and security, and runs the risk of being converted into a sort of international institute of technology or into an ineffective chapter of the International Red Cross." But he also warned that such a development might force the world "toward a concept of new centers of power upon which to build a new structure for peace."

The possibility is recognized even by some Americans. A former Ambassador to the U.N. pointed out that "When the Assembly of 132 states adopts a resolution, that action represents, as nearly as any action can in a world of separate sovereign states, the predominant public opinion of the world. It may not have the force of law, but it often has the force of prophecy." The danger exists, if such countries as the United States continue, under Nixon's strategy of benign neglect, to ignore these new forces, that the conflicts between rich and poor, strong and weak, might become more difficult of resolution through the U.N., and force the Third World into a belligerent and united stance against the great powers.

Despite their diversity, the under-developed nations share important objectives. A passionate determination to protect national identity underlies a diplomatic policy of non-alignment in the Russian-American ideological competition. In all the Third World states, economic development is the most urgent imperative. Confronted with the necessity of seeking outside aid, most have resisted subordination into neo-colonialism and have sought instead to cooperate with each other. The Latin American

Free Trade Association, the Organization of African Unity, the Arab League, and other regional associations — ranging from customs unions to common markets — have accelerated progress in many areas. Although torn with dissension and internal conflict, these associations provide a basis for a developing unity in the Third World — a contingency which offers hope that the destructive Cold War competition between the superpowers will give way to a more creative future.

The ramifications of Third World development hold far-reaching implications for the future of the European states. The harsh realities of the energy crisis in 1974, which forced curtailment of production in Europe to the extent of a three-day work week in England, underscored the continuing dependence of the European economies on the formerly colonial areas. Global interdependence is far greater in the latter half of the twentieth century than at any time in the world's history, and the imperatives to find solutions to grave problems are concomitantly greater.

23

The Industrially Advanced Nations in the Contemporary Era

THE SEARCH FOR new forms of social organization worked profound change within Europe as well as without. In the immediate post-war years each of the major nations of western Europe moved rapidly into consolidation of the welfare state. With the aid of the Marshall Plan and the security provided against further Soviet expansion by NATO, economic recovery occurred with an awesome rapidity – in West Germany it has been called a miracle. In less than a decade after the war Europe was back on her feet, although she had not regained her pre-war ascendancy in international affairs.

• England

England turned to reconstruction immediately following the defeat of Germany. In July, 1945, a national election turned the indomitable war leader, Winston Churchill, and his Conservative government out of office. Labour, led by Clement Attlee, won a mandate for sweeping internal change and advanced the British movement toward a centrally controlled economy, a direction begun but not completed before the war.

Compensating the private owners for their property, the Labour Government nationalized the coal industry and began nationalization of the steel industries, and established government control over the railroads and other segments of England's transportation facilities. But socialization of the economy stopped with nationalization of the essential primary industries — England retained a mixed economy, with ownership still largely in private hands. Government economic planning expanded England's already progressive system of social welfare — initiating a National Health Service in 1948 which provided free medical care, hospitalization, and drugs to all citizens. Educational reforms democratized public schooling and provided increased educational opportunities — the number of university students in England tripled in twenty years, creating an enormous demand for schools, teachers, and educational facilities. Government subsidies greatly increased the amount and quality of housing available to England's working classes, and social legislation provided benefits for unemployment, sickness, child care, and old-age pensions.

The expansion of government subsidized benefits meant sharply increased taxation for the British citizen. The cost of social services rose sharply, at the same time that England struggled to regain a favorable balance of trade in order to remedy the dislocations in the British economy. Yet, despite a few strident critics, the British people overwhelmingly supported England's transformation into a welfare state. Labour's reform program ended in 1951, when the Conservatives returned to power, but the Conservatives retained almost totally the changes Labour had initiated.

English democracy became stronger than ever in the post-war years. The old Liberal Party, already weak before the war, now practically disappeared, and the Labour and Conservative Parties dominated British politics. By 1951 Labour had achieved the goals it had demanded since its inception and evolved an increasingly moderate, middle-class orientation. At the same time, the Conservatives adopted much of Labour's earlier philosophy, accepting without further resistance the necessity of a government controlled economy. After the 1960s both parties operated in the moderate center of the political spectrum.

England's post-war economic revolution did not immediately solve all her economic ills, although it reduced the gap between rich and poor and advanced prosperity and security for the British people. In the 1960s England exhibited all the symptoms of economic old age. Her industrial facilities, the first to be built, required extensive modernization. The breakup of her colonial empire reduced both her access to raw materials and the availability of guaranteed markets. Her exclusion from the European Economic Community further handicapped economic growth, and her ties to the Commonwealth and to the Outer Seven (EFTA) proved less stimulating than she had hoped. In an effort to share the economic

President Charles de Gaulle. Wide World Photos.

progress which distinguished the EEC, England, after years of debate and the final consent of France, voted to become a Common Market member. Participation in the European economic union draws England inextricably into the European community and finally marks the end of her traditional reluctance to identify with Europe's destiny. Despite her economic decline after the war, England remained an industrial innovator, developing strength in such technological fields as computers, jet aircraft, and other advanced transportation facilities. Despite deepening economic anxieties in the 1970s, the discovery of vast oil reserves in the North Sea has stimulated British hopes of renewed vitality in the future.

• The Fourth French Republic

France's recovery from the devastation of the war was more difficult. For over a decade political stability proved as elusive as in the inter-war period. The end of the Vichy regime, the Nazi puppet government in France, meant that France's governmental system had to be organized anew; with overwhelming consensus, the French established the Fourth Republic. But the Fourth Republic, like the Third, retained a weak executive, with the seat of power still in the legislature. Charles de Gaulle, elected President in 1945, failed to convince French voters that constitutional revision was a necessary prerequisite to effective government and retired in frustration in 1946.

Wracked by both internal and imperial crises, the Fourth Republic proved incapable of bringing order to France. A growing Communist Party threatened revolutionary change, and the new imperial French Union was an unstable edifice from its inception. Although France made progress in economic reconstruction, nearly doubling her industrial production by 1951, the national budget remained unbalanced and the French population strenuously resisted increased taxation. Social legislation was nevertheless increased – social security, health insurance, unemployment benefits, government subsidized housing, and agricultural programs placed great strains on the economy. Between 1945 and 1958 succeeding administrations struggled to maintain stability, but cabinets fell on the average of two a year.

Imperial crises, however, finally caused the Fourth Republic's collapse. The Indo-Chinese War combined with rising inflation and continued economic instability to create grave tensions, but the colonial conflict in Algeria finally overwhelmed the government. A revolt of French Army officers in Algeria in 1958 created an extreme crisis and the French people turned once more to Charles de Gaulle for leadership. On June 1, 1958, the National Assembly voted de Gaulle dictatorial powers for six months. He immediately turned to restructuring the French political system. In September the French approved a new constitution, the basis of the Fifth French Republic. The Constitution greatly increased the power of the president, who was now elected by the people rather than by the legislature. The parliament, consisting of a National Assembly and a Senate, retained legislative control, but could be dissolved by the President and the Premier. Furthermore, in a crisis, the President could rule by executive decree upon approval of the French legislature.

● The Fifth Republic

De Gaulle, the first President of the Fifth Republic under the new Constitution, retained the executive office until 1969. He ruled with great authority, but France was still undeniably a democratic republic. Stubborn, nationalistic, often narrowminded, de Gaulle was nevertheless firmly committed to democracy and was determined to guide France toward democratic stability. Under his leadership France experienced political security and economic growth and expansion for the first time in nearly a century.

By 1962 de Gaulle had settled the Algerian crisis, although not, as many Frenchmen had assumed he would, by retaining colonial control. Instead, he granted Algeria independence and ended the drain on France's human and economic resources. In foreign relations with the western powers he pursued a firm and independent nationalistic course. His insistence on developing atomic power for France irritated the United States, already annoyed with his challenges to American predominance in Europe's defense policies. Moreover, although French statesmen had led the development of the European Economic Community, de Gaulle opposed its evolution into a politically United Europe, insisting instead upon a loose union of sovereign states – a "Europe of Fatherlands." His refusal to agree to British entry into the Common Market severely retarded progress toward supra-nationalism in Europe, an evolution necessary to the reconsolidation of power for the European continent.

De Gaulle retired in 1969. Under his successors France has maintained the stability achieved under the Fifth Republic. Failure to initiate further reforms, however, and the economic dislocations incurred in the world-wide energy crisis, have resulted in the rapid and threatening growth of the Left. In recent elections the haunting spectre of a communist victory has posed anxious questions about France's political future.

● The Rebirth of German Democracy

West Germany experienced a remarkable economic resurgence after the war. The newly established Bonn Republic was headed by the

73-year-old Konrad Adenauer, who firmly guided Germany's young democratic regime through its difficult early years. In 1963 Ludwig Erhard replaced Adenauer as Chancellor. Under Adenauer and Erhard the German government expanded social services and struggled to deepen the roots of democracy in the German population. Germany faced unique social problems in assimilating the refugees who swarmed into the western sectors from eastern Europe, placing great strains on housing and employment. Furthermore, many German people remained bitter about the division of the country, and continued to insist that the parts be reunited. But the threat of Soviet domination counteracted the possibility of any revived excess of nationalism, and by 1970, when Chancellor Willy Brandt signed the Moscow Treaty with Russia, accepting existing boundaries of all European states (but without interfering with the four-power responsibilities toward Germany), the West Germans seemed reconciled to the partition of the German nation.

By the 1970s West Germany was a thriving, energetic state, with extensive social welfare services, and a healthy capitalistic economy. In 1945 the area was an economic vacuum. Within fifteen years West Germany had more gold per capita than did the United States; the Federal Republic ranked third in the world in industrial power, and second in trading power. During that period the German currency became the most stable in Europe, and the rate of growth of her gross national product was more than double that of the United States. German technology moved into the vanguard of industrial nations and drew Germany into a position of strength in Europe's evolving economic union, which caused even France, traditionally Germany's most bitter enemy, to recognize that no viable European Union can develop without the inclusion of West Germany. Brandt's signing a non-aggression treaty with Russia in 1970 indicates that West Germany can today largely ignore the lead of the United States. Two decades after the war the western portion of Germany had moved, politically and economically, firmly into the western bloc. The middle classes came to full power, without the authoritarian ruling class of the past — aristocracy, army, and civil service — to provide its value system. For the first time Germany could genuinely try to establish the democratic process. Individuals had become citizens rather than subjects.

• Italian Reconstruction

In Italy, after Mussolini was killed in 1945, King Victor Emmanuel III abdicated in favor of his son, Humbert II. But a plebiscite in 1946 turned Italy into a republic, and Humbert II moved to Portugal. The

Constitution of the new Italian Republic vested legislative power in a bicameral assembly, composed of a Chamber of Deputies and a Senate. As in West Germany the President held largely ceremonial powers — executive authority was controlled by a cabinet and a prime minister. Numerous parties developed, from neo-fascist on the right to communist on the left, but the Church-supported, middle-of-the-road Christian Democratic Party drew more votes than any other. Italy's Communist Party, the strongest in free Europe, provided a strong challenge, because it proved to be remarkably un-revolutionary and firmly nationalistic. The socialists constantly weakened their potential by factional disputes and splits, but one or another socialist group often participated in coalitions. Although Italy has averaged more than one cabinet a year since World War II, the democratic process appears to rest on a more solid foundation than before the war. Much progress has been made in economic and social reform. The government participates in a mixed economy, a combination of government ownership, private ownership, and extensive government regulation and planning. In 1962 the entire electric power industry was nationalized. Housing projects have high priority, and many of the larger landholdings have gone into development projects, both public and private, to improve conditions in southern Italy, and the differences between northern and southern Italy gradually are disappearing.

• Europe: New Problems

While the general standard of living rose in the post-war era, by the 1970s resurgent problems were apparent in western Europe. Particularly worrisome was governmental inability to control rampant inflation. Social evolution changed family life, created demands for greater political and economic equality, and promoted a crisis of values.

Western Europe has remained a bastion of democracy and individual liberty, but the growth of communism endangers traditional values. While many argue that "Eurocommunism," the term given the nationalistic brands of French, Italian, Spanish, Portuguese and British communist creeds, is not a real danger to the survival of democracy, others insist that its triumph would destroy the European community and undermine NATO. Although Eurocommunists claim that they seek to reform society by parliamentary means and to develop their own roads to democratic socialism, their success would inevitably lead to a radical restructuring of the European states. The spread of international terrorism, particularly virulent in Italy and West Germany, has strongly reinforced fears for continued stability and vitality in the Western democracies.

• The Soviet Bloc

Besides the millions of lives lost as a result of World War II, more than 20,000,000 Russians were without housing of any kind. Probably 25 percent of the pre-war wealth of the country had been destroyed and the industrial labor force declined by more than 10,000,000. Yet the Soviet Union recovered with amazing rapidity, and within little more than a decade the Russian people had more of the basic consumer goods available than at any time in their history. Agriculture remained the most serious problem. Despite continued efforts to increase the efficiency of the Kolkhozes, agricultural production did not meet the needs of the populations, and Russia depended on large imports of grain to satisfy food demands.

To achieve such recovery required harsh discipline and the conviction that Russia's war continued. The government convinced the people that the country was in constant danger from the capitalist and imperialist enemies surrounding her and appealed to Russian nationalism to inspire the people to greater efforts. A comprehensive anti-American propaganda campaign insisted that wartime conditions must prevail until Russia could defend herself against the imperialist threat. With such incentives the government not only maintained defense spending, but in the 1950s launched an expensive but spectacular space program. At the same time she rebuilt her entire economy. The drain on Soviet economic resources prevented the country from achieving the standard of living characteristic in western Europe. But by the end of the 1960s, the Russian people enjoyed many of the material benefits of "bourgeois" society, and the grim, cruel years of the transition to communism became one more period in Russia's unhappy past.

• De-Stalinization

Politically, as well, tensions in Soviet society gradually diminished after Stalin's death in 1953. In his last years Stalin's paranoia reached a pathologic level, culminating just before his death with the threat of another purge. When Stalin died, in March 1953, fear and apprehension relaxed, but were replaced by a struggle for the succession which was not resolved until Nikita Khrushchev emerged in 1955 as the acknowledged leader of the Soviet state. In 1956, in a speech at the Twentieth Party Congress, Khrushchev astonished the world by denouncing Stalin, his tyranny, and his "cult of personality." The speech marked the beginning of a program of de-Stalinization — a relaxation of controls in Russian society.

Although Khrushchev alleviated despotism in Russia, he nevertheless reigned as a dictator until 1964. He filled party ranks with his supporters and expelled opponents from positions of power. He did not, however, execute them as Stalin had. Krushchev relaxed censorship in art and literature, but serious dissent still would not be tolerated. In 1958 Boris Pasternak won the Nobel Prize for literature for his novel, *Dr. Zhivago,* which attacked the Russian revolutionary experience. Pasternak was not permitted to accept the award and the novel was not published in Russia. But courageous Soviet writers continued to smuggle manuscripts to the West, criticizing aspects of the Soviet regime. The novelist Alexander Solzhenitzen, in *One Day in the Life of Ivan Denisovitch* and *Cancer Ward,* exposed the fundamental oppression which characterized Soviet life. The poet Yevgeny Yevtushenko attacked Soviet policies which stifle freedom of expression. Although the right to dissent has by no means been established in the Soviet Union, the very existence of such voices indicates a moderation of political tyranny in Russia and offers hope that the future will witness a further evolution toward freedom.

Khrushchev embarked on a program of economic, administrative, and cultural reform within Russia. He attempted to solve Russia's agricultural difficulties by opening up new lands to cultivation, and he initiated a program of administrative decentralization, creating regional ministries to supervise economic concerns. Both programs proved unsuccessful, and their failure helped bring about his downfall in 1964.

• Satellite Rebellion

As a result of de-Stalinization and relaxation, revolts erupted in the satellite states of Poland and Hungary. The Soviet government reacted strongly. In Poland, Wladislaw Gomulka led a series of strikes and riots which exhibited a resurgence of Polish nationalism, and seized control of the Polish government. He remained, however, unquestionably dedicated to the communist ideology, and the Russians allowed him to remain in power. The Hungarian revolution of 1956 was put down with ruthless brutality. The Hungarian revolutionaries denounced Russian supremacy and moved toward a renunciation of communism and removal of the state from the Soviet bloc. The Russians responded with savagery. Soviet troops rolled into Hungary and the free world recoiled in shock at pictures of Russian tanks gunning down students and young children whose only weapons were rocks and home-made gasoline bombs.

Although cracks in the structure of monolithic communism did indeed appear, the Soviet government demonstrated clearly in 1968 that it would not tolerate serious deviation from the Communist ideology. In 1967 the Czechoslovakian people, under the leadership of Alexander Dubcek, began a program of political liberalization. Dubcek did not intend to revise radically the Czechoslovak socialist economic system. Nevertheless, his demands for greater political freedom within Czechoslovakia antagonized the Russian government. Czechoslovakia's strategic importance in the Russian defense system meant that Russian domination of the Czech state could not relax. In the spring of 1968 Russian tanks moved into Czechoslovakia and Soviet control was forcefully reconfirmed. Dubcek was removed from office and sent into retirement in the country and a tame government put into his place.

During the decade of the 1960s Rumania achieved at least a partial independence of Soviet control. She denounced the invasion of Czechoslovakia without being herself occupied. The Sino-Soviet split improved her bargaining position, and recently she has experienced a considerable relaxation of censorship and secret police activities. Her large oil fields serve as the basis for an extensive industrial development and a Western-oriented, as well as eastern trade. In 1969 military clashes between Russians and Chinese along their common border blew long-developing ideological differences between the two countries into a serious split, and Russia has consequently found it advisable to moderate her militancy toward the West.

• Cracks in the Structure

The treaty between East and West Germany at the end of 1972 illustrated the increasing awareness among governments that détente was essential and possible. It opened the way for international acceptance of East Germany, which had been an outlaw state to the West, acknowledged only by the communist and Arab Blocs. The treaty made it possible for the western states to exchange ambassadors with East Germany before her entry into the United Nations in the Fall of 1973. Russia's acquiescence indicates a major change in attitude since the days of the Berlin Blockade.

Russia's continued strength depends in large measure, of course, on control of eastern Europe by communist parties at least friendly to, if not dominated by, Russia. Eastern Europe provides the strategic guarantee of security she deems essential for her protection. As early as 1947 the satellite countries bought one-half of Russia's total exports, and provided more than a third of her imports. When the Marshall Plan aid proved effective in the West, Russia countered in 1949 with the Council for Economic Mutual Assistance (COMECON), designed to tie the economies of the satellites to Russia. While there is no question but that the system operated to Russia's advantage, major economic growth characterized the satellites. They now produce several times their pre-war levels.

By 1956 a clearly evident movement toward local autonomy emerged and Russia chose to accept a large degree of independence among the eastern European states. Certainly the Russians must maintain some control over the area and its economies, but nationalism has proved an effective counter-force to total Russian subjugation. The communist nations of eastern Europe must be considered from now on as forces in their own right – not merely as colonial adjuncts of an all-powerful Russian state.

• The United States

Americans entered the post-war era in a mood of confidence and optimism which absorbed even the shocks of the Cold War. After Roosevelt's death in 1945, Harry Truman, a blunt, outspoken midwestern statesman, became President and steered the country through the years of adjustment following the war. In foreign affairs Truman demonstrated a strong resistance to communist expansion. In domestic affairs he attempted to extend New Deal policies and to provide more equitable justice. Americans, however, content with the changes of the Roosevelt administration, and comfortably certain that post-war prosperity would continue, defeated Truman's domestic proposals. In 1952 Americans rejected Adlai Stevenson and a Democratic social welfare platform, electing the Republican war-hero Dwight Eisenhower as President. Eisenhower retained the presidential office throughout the decade of the 1950s, a period marked by increasing affluence for the majority of Americans.

In direct opposition to the developing of central planning which even the United States insisted upon for European countries, the American government turned back toward cooperation between government and big business. The huge industrial plants which had been built by tax money during the war were now sold at a tiny fraction of cost to private interests and turned to domestic production. Middle-class complacency with accelerating economic growth bred the assumption that American prosperity would inevitably extend to every citizen, and contributed to indifference to reform. Fear of the communist ideology, now bolstered by Russia's expansive power, became pathological, and caused Americans to identify all reform with "creeping socialism."

Senator Joseph McCarthy of Wisconsin convinced the majority of Americans that the Democratic Party was engaged in a conspiracy to overthrow the American Way of Life. McCarthyism resulted in a witch hunt so extreme that by 1953 an inevitable reaction among enlightened leadership set in, which ultimately ended McCarthy's support, and permitted the country to turn again to an examination of surviving inequalities in American social and economic life.

The most obvious issue was the place of the nation's disinherited blacks. Although President Truman's civil rights program of 1948 found little support at that time, it did awaken some American leaders to the problem of Negro inequality. Congressional rejection left the matter to the courts, and in 1954 the Supreme Court ruled against continued segregation in southern schools. The Supreme Court decision marked the beginning of an awakening of black political, social, and economic consciousness. The failure of the administration to implement the decision led to the rise of effective individual black leaders, such as Martin Luther King, Jr., who adopted Mohandas Gandhi's tactics and preached non-violent resistance to prejudice. The success of economic boycotts, sit-ins and civil rights marches generated fear among the white, middle-class establishment and led to ugly, violent confrontation, riots, and murder.

• The 1960s: Polarization and Paranoia

The presidential election of 1960 revealed a sharp division in the American people. The Republican candidate, Richard Nixon, known primarily for his support of McCarthyism and his Eisenhower economics, was devoid of charisma. His opponent, John Kennedy, a dynamic young Senator from Massachusetts, led the Democrats to victory on a reform platform. For the moment it appeared that the reform ethos had once again emerged as a dominant strain in American political thought. But Kennedy's clarion call to Americans to put into practice the rhetoric of the American Constitution ushered in a period of social conflict and violence, culminating in a series of assassinations which profoundly shocked the population. Kennedy himself was assassinated in 1963; Martin Luther King, Jr., a leader of the black civil rights movement, in 1967; and Robert Kennedy, the former President's brother, and himself a presidential candidate, in 1968. The profound split in American opinion, centering on the participation of blacks in the benefits of the American system, became increasingly apparent.

Vice-President Lyndon Johnson quickly asserted himself as President upon Kennedy's death. He used all his power with Congress to reduce taxes on less affluent Americans, and to pass the Civil Rights Act of 1964. The Civil Rights Act provided the federal government power to guarantee voting rights, equal educational and job opportunities, and use of public facilities to all citizens. He proposed his own "War on Poverty" program and pressured Congress into establishing the machinery and appropriating money to implement it. The people responded by giving him the greatest landslide victory in American history in the 1964 election.

Johnson proposed in his State-of-the-Union Message that Americans build "the Great Society," and his first Congress passed a series of bills which laid the foundations: federal aid to education; medical assistance for over-65 year olds; abolition of poll tax, literacy tests, and other methods of preventing voting by blacks; and cabinet level posts for Housing and Urban Affairs and for Transportation.

But the split in society became more evident during these years. A series of massive civil rights demonstrations and vicious riots spread across the nation. In Los Angeles, Cleveland, Chicago, and New York, particularly violent confrontations occurred. Urban whites in the northern cities responded with bitter prejudice and hatred for the blacks who seemed to endanger their status. At the same time the Johnson administration increased the number of Americans in Vietnam by more than a quarter of a million in one year, and growing numbers of the voters turned away from both Johnson and his conception of the Great Society. Escalation of the war in Vietnam exacerbated the already obvious schism between the middle-class establishment and growing numbers of dissident minority groups.

• The Nixon Years

Richard Nixon led the Republicans to victory in 1968 on a platform of law and order and withdrawal from Vietnam. Although Nixon failed in both promises, and continuing frustration threatened to rip the entire fabric of American society, a growing conservative sentiment brought the Republicans back to office in 1972. The 1973 end of the Vietnam conflict was overshadowed, however, by the Watergate scandals, a long series of revelations of presidential complicity in theft, political chicanery and obstruction of justice which resulted in Nixon's near impeachment and resignation in 1974.

Strident demands from still-alienated segments of society – blacks, women and other minority groups – produced profound social change in the 1970s. Their very success, however, created a backlash and the country experienced a marked shift to the conservative right. Although the voters rejected President Gerald Ford's bid for reelection in 1976, primarily because of the Watergate scandals, the new Democratic President, Jimmy Carter, was remarkably conservative in many ways and by 1978 American taxpayers were in rebellion against spiraling inflation and increasing taxation in support of continuing high government expenditures.

American discontents reflected a pervasive disenchantment throughout the Western world, indicating a cultural crisis of threatening proportions. Europe and the United States share the struggle against possible totalitarianism – either from the right or the left. Both areas face hard choices in determining the future patterns of western development.

In foreign policy Americans showed a greater willingness to abandon outdated concepts and to reassess their position. In the years following World War II, containment of communism was a valid policy, particularly for a world disillusioned by the failure of the West to restrain the forces of aggression through appeasement. The Vietnam War, however, invalidated the basic assumptions of the containment policy, forcing Americans to recognize that social revolution in the emerging nations cannot be equated with communist expansion. Moreover, it challenged America's belief that her resources were infinite and brought the recognition that the United States neither can, nor wants to be, the world's policeman.

- ● **East-West Rapprochement**

As the Cold War moderated into détente, American statesmen faced the necessity of a drastic revision of foreign policy. In 1971 Americans suffered the shock of international opposition to their policy, when the United Nations voted to admit Red China to membership. Within a year President Nixon had faced the realities of changed world conditions, and opened relations with the Chinese Communist state. While Nixon's visit to China served primarily as a beginning of relations between the two countries, that in itself signified a vast change in American policy, a recognition that the United States deplored its increasing isolation. Nixon's trip to Russia later in 1972 resulted in more immediate and tangible agreements. The attitudes on both sides showed marked change from those of 1968 and demonstrated a drive toward mutual self-interest. The Russians wanted American trade and a generally closer relationship with the West, which would permit them to share in technological developments and ease Cold War tensions. Nixon wanted to gain support for his tough line in Vietnam, where he had recently mined Haiphong Harbor and increased the heavy bombing of North Vietnam. Perhaps both wished to convince the world that there were still only two superpowers and that they could arrange world affairs by themselves.

In a series of highly publicized agreements Russia and the United States agreed to limit strategic nuclear weapons and to continue the Strategic Arms Limitation Talks (SALT). Although the agreement left both countries with sufficient nuclear arms to destroy human life, it did mark a distinct improvement in relations. Other agreements provided for the two countries to pool their resources to improve health and to protect the environment, and to rendezvous Russian and American spaceships in orbit in 1975, using crews trained together in both countries, and ships rigged to mutual compatibility in all essentials, such as radio frequencies and docking systems.

Perhaps more significant than all of the signed agreements, however, was the simple fact that the heads of two heretofore incompatible social systems examined the wishes and needs of both, found that they could agree on mutually advantageous matters while peaceably disagreeing on others. Nixon's visits to Peking and then to Moscow marked the inauguration of a new course in American foreign policy, one moved by the spirit of cooperation rather than antagonism.

• Contemporary Perspectives: The Scientific Revolution

Perhaps the most striking of the distinguishing features of twentieth century civilization is the advance in science and technology. The rapid acceleration of technological change, stimulated by the extension of scientific knowledge, has provoked a sweeping social revolution and profoundly affected politics and economics. The crises of the twentieth century — war, revolution, depression — have all had roots in the technological revolution which began in the nineteenth century, but dynamically increased since the middle of the present century.

There is little doubt that technological developments have greatly benefited mankind. Man's ability to manipulate and control his environment is greater than ever before in history. Bacteriology, microbiology, pharmacology, virology, and awesome progress in surgical technique conquered many traditional killers, while increased knowledge in preventive medicine and nutrition now control formerly lethal diseases which were still prevalent at the beginning of the century.

Transportation and communication facilities, particularly since the Second World War, have produced instantaneous communication with even the most remote corners of the globe. Continental and intercontinental travel have become commonplace. Consequently, the world has, in effect, become smaller, and events occurring half-way around the globe send repercussions not only to neighboring nations, but to the farthest corners of the earth. In the contemporary era, the interdependence of nations cannot be evaded nor denied.

New modes of production and increases in agricultural efficiency have brought material comfort to the majority in all of the industrialized nations. The inescapable evidence of a marked increase in the standard of living has produced the desire, in the under-developed nations of the world, to acquire equal scientific and industrial strength and the resulting material benefits for their own populations, and has been a major stimulus in generating nationalism in the Third World.

Perhaps the most spectacular developments in science have occurred in the field of space exploration. Formerly a subject only for science fiction, manned flight in space has extended knowledge in numerous areas, particularly in discovering the origins of the universe. The Space Age began in 1957, when the Russians launched *Sputnik,* a capsule which became the earth's first man-made satellite. *Sputnik* touched off a space-race between the Soviet Union and the United States which dominated the decade of the 1960s, affecting education, defense, and every area of scientific endeavor. In December, 1968, the United States sent the first space-crew into orbit around the moon and the following year the whole world watched as Neil Armstrong stepped down onto moon territory. His comment, "That's one small step for a man, one giant leap for mankind," articulated clearly the implications of man's victory over space.

• The Problems of Scientific Advance

But scientific progress has not been an unmitigated blessing. New methods of military defense obviously threaten the survival of mankind. The world first witnessed an atomic mushroom cloud as it hung over Hiroshima and Nagasaki in 1945. The residual horrors of atomic warfare were only gradually discovered as the poisoning effects of radioactive fallout became known. In 1952 the United States announced a new and even more powerful hydrogen bomb, and both Russia and the United States experimented with chemical and bacterial warfare. As other nations built atomic arsenals, the likelihood increased that a nuclear war would

The earth as seen from the moon. Wide World Photos.

destroy all life on the planet. The fear of a nuclear holocaust has diminished somewhat with the realization of the possibility of human genocide, but until strict controls over nuclear buildup are implemented, the ominous threat remains.

Extended life expectancy and the control of disease has caused a staggering increase in the world's population. A United Nations Conference on World Population held in Rome in 1954 established that the world at that time held 2.5 billion people, and predicted that there would be 6 billion by the year 2000. The figure is probably conservative.

Statisticians today generally believe that by the turn of the century the world's population will begin to double every generation. Thus by 2025 there would be 12 billion people, or four times as many as presently exist, and 25 years later the figure would be 24 billion. These estimates are given credence by the fact that in many areas of the world (including Mexico) the population is already doubling every generation. Death rates decline while birth rates rise, despite deliberate governmental policies in some countries to control population growth – Japan's government shortly after World War II legalized and encouraged abortion.

The population explosion created overwhelming social and economic problems. Particularly in the underdeveloped areas of the world, food production has lagged behind population increase, and thousands suffer from starvation and disease. The poorer classes in India consume only about 25 percent as many calories as the wealthier classes in the United States. But figures concerning other consumption are even more startling. Per capita, Americans use 20 times more energy than Indians, 80 times as much iron, and two-thirds of the world's total oil production. While the increase in population is rapidly depleting the world's resources, associated problems absorb the attention of national authorities. Major crises in over-crowded cities and a sky-rocketing increase in the crime rate are directly related to the demographic rise. Population control is consequently one of the contemporary era's most insistent imperatives.

Excessive population growth is also a major factor in pollution of every kind – air, water, noise. Many of the world's lakes and rivers have already lost all plant and fish life through discharge of poisonous wastes into them from factories, industrial complexes, and sewage lines. Smog and air pollution have turned whole cities into hazardous living areas. Noise levels in the large cities, and increasingly where supersonic planes fly, have reached danger levels. The search for new sources of energy has endangered wide geographical areas, and entire species of wildlife are threatened with extinction as man, in attempting to control his environment, faces the very real danger of destroying it.

● The Intellectual Revolution

Rapidly accelerating social change has produced a growing tendency to challenge traditional concepts. Culturally and intellectually, the questioning of western values and priorities which had emerged in the 1920s and 1930s accelerated in the 1960s and 1970s. As material comfort reached the majority in the advanced nation, it became increasingly clear that affluence did not insure spiritual satisfaction. Throughout the western states a rejection of traditional patterns of thought, which eqated progress with Gross National Product, gained momentum. Cultural critics condemn the environmental and spiritual spoliation caused by modern technology, and decry the materialism which pervades western society. They argue that fear of a nuclear holocaust is an ever-present reality, but that industrial potential threatens life and freedom in subtler and equally dangerous ways.

As in the seventeenth and eighteenth centuries, the scientific revolution has produced an intellectual revolution in which serious thinkers seek to find a coherent body of principles to replace the invalidated former guidelines. Organized religion, under the leadership of theologians such as Karl Barth, Paul Tillich, and Pope John XXIII, is in a period of flux as it attempts to combat secularism and reconstruct religious doctrines meaningful to modern man. In philosophy, Existentialism has attempted to respond to the absurdities of contemporary life and to re-emphasize, despite the anguish of twentieth-century life, human freedom and dignity.

But the most profound challenge to the fundamental precepts of western civilization emerged in the 1960s in the ranks of western youth. A dissident younger generation, influenced by the obvious contradictions between their parents' rhetoric and practice, burst into rebellion as they rejected established creeds and life-styles. Student riots and demonstrations in Paris, Tokyo, Berlin, and all over the United States manifested a violent rejection of the established order. The movement alienated many of the older generation, who felt that their efforts to preserve western civilization against the onslaughts of depression, communism, and fascism have not been appreciated by their children, raised in greater comfort than any generation in history. But the older generation as well is affected by the proven validity of the criticism.

• Confronting the Future

Until the present century Europe and the West stood in the vanguard of progress. The experiences of two world wars, the emergence of a third world bloc of young nations, and the perplexities of an advanced technological society have necessitated fundamental adjustments in western social organization, and in political and economic thought. Neither the more advanced western states nor the emerging nations will abandon the undeniable benefits or material comforts of industrialization, but the technology must be controlled if civilization is to survive. The western world, the source of the ideas and knowledge which created the technology, consequently bears an awesome responsibility. Leadership in solving the problems of industrial society must come from the nations which gave it birth. If scientific knowledge and industrialization are not to become Frankenstein monsters, destroying their creators, then the western nations must awaken to the exigencies of modern civilization. In the contemporary world Europe and her step-children, Russia and the United States, face a formidable task: assuring the survival of the human race.

Suggestions for Further Reading

The best work for understanding the contemporary period is Geoffrey Barraclough, *An Introduction to Contemporary History* (1967).

Europe's regeneration after 1945 is discussed in Maurice Crouzet, *The European Renaissance* (1970) and R. Mayne, *The Recovery of Europe* (1970). Werner J. Feld, *The European Community in World Affairs* (1976) analyzes Europe's post-war international role. J.W. Nystrom and G.W. Hoffman, *The Common Market* (1976) and R. Gurland and A. MacLean, *The Common Market* (1974) describe the prospects and challenges of European integration.

The Cold War is the subject of W. LaFeber, *America, Russia and the Cold War* (1968), and David Rees, *The Age of Containment: The Cold War* (1967). Daniel Yergin, *Shattered Peace: The Origins of the Cold War and the National Security State* (1977) and Richard J. Barnet, *The Giants: Russia and America* (1977) discuss relations between the super powers from Cold War origins to tenuous *détente*.

For France see Gordon Wright, *France in Modern Times* (1962), Brian Crozier, *DeGaulle* (1973), Philip M. Williams and Martin Harrison, *Politics and Society in DeGaulle's Republic* (1973), and Daniel Singer, *Prelude to Revolution: France in May 1968* (1970). Excellent because it is brief and cogent is Raymond Aron, *France: Steadfast and Changing* (1960). Simon Serfaty, *France, DeGaulle and Europe* (1968) is a concise survey of DeGaulle's controversial foreign policy.

The continuing crises of parliamentary democracy in Italy are delineated in Elizabeth Wiskemann, *Italy Since 1945* (1971), Norman Kagan, *A Political History of Postwar Italy* (1966), Giuseppi Mammarella, *Italy after Facism: A Political History 1943-1965* (1966), and Dante Germino and Stefano Passigli, *The Government and Politics of Contemporary Italy* (1968). F. Roy Willis, *Italy Chooses Europe* (1971), is a readable study of Italy's external relations.

For Great Britain a clear, penetrating and impartial general survey is C.J. Bartlett, *A History of Postwar Britain 1945-74* (1977). Frank Stacey, *British Government, 1966-75: Years of Reform* (1975) presents a rather hopeful account of developments, while a more pessimistic view is found in Stephen Haseler, *The Death of British Democracy* (1976). Harold Wilson, *A Personal Record: The Labour Government, 1964-70* (1971) is a first-hand account by a significant participant. Britain's relationships with the super powers and with the Commonwealth are well covered by Joseph Frankel, *British Foreign Policy 1945-1973* (1975) and Elizabeth Barker, *Britain and a Divided Europe 1945-70* (1971).

Analysis of post-Nazi Germany include Carl Landauer, *Illusions and Dilemmas* (1969), Alfred Grosser, *Germany in our Time* (1971), Gunther Klass, *West Germany: An Introduction* (1976). Jean Smith, *Germany Beyond the Wall* (1969) is quite a readable study of East Germany. Konrad Adenauer, *Memoirs 1945-53* (1966) is a first-hand account by West Germany's first Chancellor. Terence Prettie, *Willy Brandt: Portrait of a Statesman* (1974) is a fascinating study.

Alexander Werth, *Russia: Hopes and Fears* (1969) and John W. Strong, ed., *The Soviet Union under Brezhnev and Kosygin* (1971) provide excellent introductions to post-Stalin Russia. Russia's relations with eastern Europe are covered adequately by Harry Schwartz, *Eastern Europe in the Soviet Shadow* (1973) and Roger Pethybridge, ed., *The Development of the Communist Bloc* (1965). Thomas W. Wolfe, *Soviet Power and Europe, 1945-1970* (1970) deals with a broader context.

Two excellent general surveys of the United States since World War II are Carl Degler, *Affluence and Anxiety* (1975) and William Leuchtenburg, *A Troubled Feast* (1973). Eric Goldman, *The Crucial Decade and After* (1960) focuses on the immediate post-war years, and William O'Neill, *Coming Apart* (1971) treats the decade of the sixties. Two aspects of exciting and significant social change can be examined in William H. Chafe, *The American Woman: Her Changing Social, Economic, and Political Roles, 1920-1970* (1972) and Malcolm Little, with Alex Haley, *The Autobiography of Malcolm X* (1965).

Barbara Ward, *The Rich Nations and the Poor Nations* (1962) and Vera Michelas Dean, *The Nature of the Non-Western World* (1964) are excellent introductions to the Third World. An acquaintance with individual areas can be obtained from the following: F. Tannenbaum, *Ten Keys to Latin America* (1963); Zbigniew Brzezinski, *The Fragile Blossom: Crisis and Change in Japan* (1972); Francis FitzGerald, *Fire in the Lake: The Vietnamese and the Americans in Vietnam* (1972); Jacques Guillermaz, *The Chinese Communist Party in Power, 1949-1976* (1976); M.N. Srinivas, et. al., *Dimensions of Social Change in India* (1978); Ali A. Mazrui and Jasu H. Patel, eds., *Africa in World Affairs* (1973). The story of the Arabs and Israelis and their continuing conflict may be most interestingly studied by reading two excellent autobiographies: Anwar el-Sadat, *In Search of Identity* (1977) and *Abba Eban* (1977).

THE NINETEENTH CENTURY

DEATH OF AN OLD WORLD, 1914-1945

GENESIS OF A NEW WORLD, 1945 TO THE PRESENT